Reading
a Source Book

Reading
a Source Book
Edited by Don Drummond and
Edna Wignell

Heinemann Educational Books
LONDON

372.36
DRu

Heinemann Educational Books Ltd
22 Bedford Square, London WC1B 3HH

LONDON EDINBURGH MELBOURNE AUCKLAND
HONG KONG SINGAPORE KUALA LUMPUR NEW DELHI
IBADAN LUSAKA NAIROBI JOHANNESBURG
EXETER (NH) KINGSTON PORT OF SPAIN

ISBN 0-435-10261-3
Original edition © Primary Education, Australia 1975, 1977
This revised edition © Heinemann Educational Books Ltd 1979
First published in Great Britain 1979

British Library C.I.P. Data
Reading: a Source Book
1. Reading (Elementary) — Study and teaching
I. Drummond, Don II. Wignell, Edna
372.4 LB1573

Typeset by Spectrum Typesetting Ltd., and
printed and bound in Great Britain by Biddles of Guildford

CONTENTS

ACKNOWLEDGEMENTS

Much of the material included in this book first appeared in the journal *Primary Education* (Melbourne) of which Don Drummond is editor.

Reading: A Source Book was first published in Australia and has been revised and adapted for the UK by Bridie Raban, Lecturer in Education at the University of Reading.

Reading in the Primary School

The Child

We teach children, not reading. Any system that does not consider the *particular* group of children and *each child in that group* first is pseudoscientific in its approach. And only a teacher can know the children she teaches — and know them she *must* before any significant gains can be accomplished.[1]

The Teacher

Students spend time figuring out their teachers' beliefs and usually have a pretty accurate view of them, often despite what the teachers say themselves. If you don't believe that reading and writing are important human activities your students will know it and tend to feel the same way you do. If you don't believe your students can learn to read with ease then the students will know that too, and question their own abilities. People who don't read or write themselves with any frequency or joy have a hard time getting others to read and write. It is difficult to teach people to value what you yourself do not value.[2]

The Method

There has been a lot of controversy in the past about how children learn to read. As time goes by, and as the results of more and more research studies become available, it has become increasingly evident that there is no one 'best' way of learning to read and that almost every method practised can be successful. Sometimes it is not so much the method used as it is the teacher, his personality, and his 'rapport' with a child. There are all sorts of factors involved in learning to read. But the one important point that emerges from this controversial field is that the child best learns how to read not so much by adapting to the methods of the teacher but by having the methods adapted to him. If the teacher knows a number of ways in which a child can learn to read then he is in a far better position to help than the teacher who knows only one way. Furthermore, the child will best learn to read from the teacher who has both a close relationship with the child and who knows how to localise the difficulties the child might be having and devise activities to help overcome those difficulties.[3]

1 Stages of Reading

Learning to read is fundamental to the social and intellectual development of the child. The provision of a sound foundation in basic reading skill areas is a key function of the primary school. In recent years teachers have become concerned with a theoretical framework within which materials, methods and the needs of individual children may be meaningfully related. In the development of reading skill it is possible to identify three relatively distinct stages:

☐ Readiness
☐ Dependence
☐ Independence (Requiring skill consolidation)
                            (Requiring the effective utilization of skills)

A. Readiness

The larger part of this period is spent in the pre-school years where the school environment has no influence. The development of reading skills is largely dependent upon the level of readiness for learning and the extent to which the school can identify and cater for differences in individual levels of readiness.

The following factors are essential to reading readiness:

☐ Adequate physical development; visual/auditory refinement; discrimination.
☐ Accuracy in pronunciation and enunciation.
☐ A wide range of environmental experiences.
☐ A reasonable command of spoken English: vocabulary, sentence structure, etc.
☐ Facility in the use of ideas.
☐ A keen interest in reading and associated activities.

How the beginner satisfies these requirements depends on his intellectual, physical and emotional maturity and his background of environmental experience. In order to cater for the wide range of individual levels of development, the school must provide for:

☐ Language enrichment.
☐ The development of motor co-ordination.
☐ Accuracy in discrimination.
☐ A sense of reason.

B. Dependence

During the first school years the development of reading ability centres around the acquisition of mechanical skills related to two broad areas of instruction.

☐ *Sight vocabulary*: the pool of words recognized on sight.
☐ *Word attack skills*: the methods of unlocking the pronunciation of words. These are initially of a phonic nature but later broaden to include the use of sight vocabulary, experience, contextual clues, intelligent guessing and so on.

In addition, at this stage of a child's development it is possible to define *precisely* the vocabulary which should be found in suitable reading material. It will include all words within the sight vocabulary pool as well as phonetically regular words capable of analysis through the use of word attack skills.

No particular teaching method is presupposed. A sight vocabulary pool will build up regardless of the method used and, as it increases, its limits will become more difficult to define.

Children who achieve similar reading age scores on a comprehension type test are not necessarily of identical reading ability. One child's performance level may have been attained through the use of a well developed sight vocabulary and restricted word attack skills, while another performance may have centred around the reverse set of skills.

When a sight pool of approximately 500 words is combined with effective word attack skills a *vocabulary explosion occurs* and the development of reading ability is no longer dependent on rigid control of methods and material. A major step towards reading independence has been taken.

```
                    VOCABULARY EXPLOSION

    Growth of                                    Growth of sight
   word attack skills                              vocabulary


                        Language Experience


            The significance of the diagram lies in the
            relative development of the two basic skill
            areas, sight vocabulary and word attack. At
            this stage overall reading ability is a multi-
            plicative function of these two levels of
            growth.
```

C. Independence (requiring skill consolidation)

When the vocabulary explosion occurs, word recognition is no longer a major problem. The skills developed during the period of dependence now require systematic consolidation through guided reading experience.

There is a need, however, to recognize three possible levels of function:

Leisure Reading — The material chosen will equate approximately to the child's sight vocabulary level. There will be little need for recourse to word attack skills.

Class Work — For effective function at this level, use must be made of total word power (sight vocabulary and word attack skills).

Maximum Performance — Satisfactory performance at this level requires the employment of all reading skills developed — sight vocabulary, word attack, comprehension, fluency and speed of reading, etc.

The three working levels are separate but inter-related. They move up the reading age scale together. A distortion of this *profile* can give a valuable guide to areas of emphasis needed in remedial instruction.

D. Independence (requiring effective utilization of skills)

Once basic skills have been acquired and practised to the point of competence, reading becomes a multi-purpose tool which is merged into the general field of English. Instructional emphasis should now be placed on the further development and refinement of mature skills:

□ *Comprehension* — Literal meaning, inference, appreciation, evaluation.

□ *Locational Skills* — Appropriate sources of information and their use in reference.

□ *Study Skills* — Summaries, skimming, speed reading, specific subject fields.

□ *Language* — Development and enrichment.

Because of the multiplicity of skills involved, a single reading age is not a truly meaningful indication of development.

The effective independent reader does not utilize his reading skills one at a time or step by step. He combines skills, abilities and understanding much as an expert swimmer uses strokes, breathing and timing techniques. In addition he brings his interests, his attitudes, his reading habits and his tastes with him to the printed page.

The teacher's task is to guide and direct these skills to effective use.

2 Reading Readiness

There can be no decisive answer to the question 'When is a child ready for reading?' because there is no single criterion that applies to all children or to all learning situations. Children grow towards readiness for reading at different rates and vary widely in the various abilities, skills and understanding which make for reading readiness; again, reading methods and materials differ from classroom to classroom affecting the threshold requirements of reading.[1]

A. Readiness

Reading readiness has been defined as 'a state of general *maturity* which allows a child to read without excess difficulty' (Harris, *How to Increase Reading Ability*). Physical, social, emotional, experiental, linguistic and mental maturity should be considered.

When planning a pre-reading programme it is important to *fit the programme to the child* rather than the child to the programme. Therefore it is the school's responsibility to ascertain the child's readiness on entry.

It is not possible to gauge the relative importance of such factors as intelligence, home background, emotional maturity, language development and nursery-school experience, especially when researchers and experts provide contradictory information. Therefore a summary of some recent research findings and the opinions of various practitioners are included in Chapter 9 to assist teachers' application of theory to practice.

The following growth areas can be evaluated: (Some can be tested on entry to school, and others will be revealed either in home/nursery-school reports, or during the first months at school.)

1. Social and Emotional Readiness

☐ Is the child secure with the teacher and the other children?
☐ Is he willing to participate and co-operate in class and group activities?
☐ Does he use his initiative?
☐ Can he carry out plans, and concentrate on an activity for some time?
☐ Is he responsible and independent in taking out, using and putting away materials?

2. Experiential Background

☐ Has the child attended nursery- or play-school? For how long? What kind of programme?
☐ Has he a foreign language background?
☐ Is his home situation secure?
☐ Has the child had contact with books, people, places?
☐ If both parents work, what provision is made for his supervision?

3. Language Development

☐ Has the child a wide vocabulary?
☐ Can he describe his experiences? Can he describe them in sentences?
☐ Can he participate in discussion?
☐ Does he speak fluently and clearly? (If he has a speech problem report immediately for diagnosis and re-mediation.)
☐ Can he retell a story in correct sequence?
☐ Can he interpret a picture?

4. Health and Physical Development

☐ Does the child enjoy good general health?
☐ Are hearing and vision normal? (If not, report immediately for correction.)
☐ Is attendance regular?
☐ Has he achieved physical control and muscular co-ordination? Eye-hand co-ordination?
☐ Can he maintain eye focus?

5. Laterality, Directionality and Body Image

- ☐ Is handedness established?
- ☐ Which eye does he favour?
- ☐ Which eye-hand combination does he favour?
- ☐ Which foot is preferred?
- ☐ Can he draw a line on the board from right to left, up and down?
- ☐ Can he identify his forehead, elbow, etc?
- ☐ Can he touch his nose with his right hand, etc?

6. Interest in Print and Books

- ☐ Can the child recognize his own name in print?
- ☐ Can he recognize print in familiar situations — notices, traffic signs, breakfast food packets, etc?
- ☐ Does he know how to handle books in the library corner?
- ☐ Does he choose to 'read' regularly from picture books and experience books?
- ☐ Does he respond with enjoyment when the teacher reads stories?

7. Following Directions

- ☐ Can the child carry out instructions in sequential order?
- ☐ Can he remember sequences? (Rhythm patterns, series of movements, numbers, words, sounds.)
- ☐ Can he recall and retell story sequences?

8. Visual Perception and Concept Development

- ☐ Can the child detect likenesses and differences in objects, pictures, colours, shapes, sizes?
- ☐ Can he detect internal differences or differences in details of pictures or designs?
- ☐ Can he detect reversal of objects?
- ☐ Can he successfully complete jig-saw puzzles and inset boards?
- ☐ Can he classify objects into categories?
- ☐ Can he make comparisons?
- ☐ Can he supply missing details?
- ☐ Can he differentiate between letters of the alphabet? (Appearance only.)

☐ Can he differentiate between combinations of letters? (Appearance only.)

☐ After looking at a display of items, shapes or letters, can he remember one that has been removed?

☐ After observing a sequence of pictures, shapes, letters, etc, can he place them in correct order? (From a jumbled pile.)

9. Tactile, Haptic-Kinaesthetic Equivalence

☐ Can the child identify common objects in a covered box by touch only?

☐ Can he match textures in a covered box with those held in the hand?

☐ Can he identify a shape in a covered box by recognition of shapes on a table?

☐ Can he touch an object and draw it without seeing it?

10. Auditory Perception

☐ Can the child discriminate between sounds in everyday life? In listening games and exercises?

☐ Can he respond to music? (Tempo, pitch, tone, rhythm.)

☐ Can he reproduce a series of sounds, number or letter sequences? Can he tell when one is missing?

☐ Can he play accumulative games, 'I went to the zoo and I saw . . .'?

☐ Can he hear initial sounds in words?

☐ Can he hear rhyming sounds, ending sounds, middle sounds in words?

☐ Can he analyse the position of a sound in a word?

☐ Can he combine two (or more) sounds?

B. Assessment of Reading Readiness

1. School Entry Screening Tests

Tests for children entering school provide information on their strengths and weaknesses, thus enabling the school to provide individual programmes of developmental training. Children with special difficulties are discovered early, and (hopefully) failure is averted. Children who have already started reading can be given a reading skills programme.

The formulation of a School Entry Screening Test is an exercise in selection. There are literally hundreds of items that can be included. However, it is impractical to have an extensive testing programme because children are unfamiliar with the teachers and the school, and the time taken for testing, scoring and evaluating can often be put to better use. If information is compiled from reports (parents' and nursery-school teachers') obtained at the end of the preceding year, it will be easier to select areas that need testing.

Two areas that should not be neglected are the various aspects of language development and auditory perception. Reading is a language skill, and auditory perception plays a very important part in the acquisition of language. Perhaps, in the past, more attention has been paid to maturity in various aspects of visual perception, some of which have little bearing on the intitial learning of reading. The following references will provide a guide for selection.

Further Reading

Marie M. Clay, *Reading: The Patterning of Complex Behaviour* (Heinemann Educational).

Tests of Reading Readiness and Achievement (Reading Aids Series, International Reading Association, Delaware).

K. de Hirsch, J. Jansky and W. Langford, *Predicting Reading Failure* (Harper and Row).

A. E. Tansley, *Reading and Remedial Reading* (Routledge and Kegan Paul).

J. A. Downing and D. V. Thackray, *Reading Readiness* (Hodder and Stoughton for the United Kingdom Reading Association).

2. Reports

A report on each child, provided by the parents (interview and/or questionnaire) and the nursery-school teacher, is valuable when used in conjunction with School Entry Screening Tests. The experience of children from widely differing backgrounds should be considered in relation to their achievements in a testing situation. Experiences and backgrounds vary widely:

☐ A child from an isolated farm travelling by bus to a large area-school; an immigrant child from a non-English speaking home; a child with both parents in professional occupations, who has spent two years at nursery-school; a child alone in the home all day (or caring for younger

children) while both parents work.
☐ Nursery- and play-school programmes vary from fairly structured to totally informal. Some nurseries provide a great deal of perceptual and motor training, especially for the older children, and those who are in their second year of attendance. Many have facilities and equipment superior to that which is provided in schools.

3. Teacher Observation and Informal Testing

Most researchers report that teachers are usually fairly accurate in assessing reading readiness. Observation and informal testing are valuable aspects of the pre-reading programme. Checklists of items, selected from the foregoing list, can be made, and each child's progress can be charted as maturity in various areas is noticed.

4. Formal Testing

Some commercially prepared readiness programmes include tests which can be used at appropriate stages.

Formal tests may be used to supplement (not replace) the teacher's tests and observations.

Thackray Reading Readiness Profiles (Hodder and Stoughton).

Gates-MacGinitie Reading Tests: Readiness Skills (Teachers College Press, New York, NFER act as UK agents).

Murphy-Durrell Reading Readiness Analysis (Harcourt, Brace and World, Inc.).

(See also P. D. Pumfrey, *Reading: Tests and Assessment Techniques*, (Hodder and Stoughton).

The behaviour that should be observed on entry to school depends on several factors — among them the individual child's past development, the programme provided in the classroom, and the type of reading programme for which the child is being prepared. There is certainly no single set sequence of skills required for beginning reading because different programmes demand different skills.[2]

C. Pre-Reading: A Developmental Programme

It seems certain that abilities such as auditory, visual, form perception, etc, are necessary in the reading process. But there is no set combination. Different children tend to develop different combinations, depending on what abilities they have. Some children, with poor visual discrimination, learn to read by using their auditory and kinaesthetic abilities; others with poor auditory discrimination, learn to read by using their powers of visual perception to the full. There are possibly as many ways of learning to read as there are children.[3]

A programme for the development of reading readiness can be planned (for those who need it) based on children's needs as shown by reports, entry screening tests, observation and informal testing.

An ongoing programme of activities and an interesting environment are important in the provision of a rich background of ideas and language stimulation which are an excellent basis for learning to read:

☐ Creative art, craft, music and drama activities;
☐ Opportunities to play, explore and discover with mathematics and science materials;
☐ Appreciation and enjoyment of poetry and stories;
☐ Construction and dramatic play with toys, blocks, household equipment, etc;
☐ Exercises using large and small physical education equipment;
☐ Caring for pets and plants.

In a book of this nature it is impossible to list all the activities that could be included in a developmental programme so the following references and resources are included to assist with selection.

Further Reading: Various Aspects

The following are useful for ideas on *many* aspects of pre-reading:

Marie M. Clay, *Reading: The Patterning of Complex Behaviour* (Heinemann Educational).

A.E. Tansley, *Reading and Remedial Reading* (Routledge and Kegan Paul).

J.A. Downing and D.V. Thackray, *Reading Readiness* (Hodder and Stoughton).

Marion Monroe and Bernice Rogers, *Foundations for Reading: Informal Pre-Reading Procedures* (Scott Foresman).

Joan Dean, *Reading, Writing and Talking* (A. & C. Black).

N.C. Kephart, *The Slow Learner in the Classroom* (Charles E. Merrill).

M. and J.B. Ebersole and N.C. Kephart, *Steps to Achievement for the Slow*

Learner (Charles E. Merrill).

C. Walker, *Pre-Reading Skills* (Ward Lock).

G. Wagner and M. Hosier, *Reading Games: Strengthening Reading Skills through Instructional Games* (Teachers Publishing Corporation).

John M. Hughes, *Beginning Reading* (Evans).

Materials

Joyce Morris (ed.), 'Language in Action Resource Books — Pre-literacy Level', *The Macmillan Language Project* (Macmillan).

A.E. Tansley, *Thinking and Learning Series* (E.J. Arnold).

A.E. Tansley and G. Davies, *Perceptual Training Pack* (E.J. Arnold).

M.B. Lorton, *Workjobs* (Addison-Wesley).

D.H. Stott, *Flying Start* and *Extension Kit* (Holmes McDougall).

Betty Root, *Reading Games* (E.J. Arnold).

C. Walker, *Pre-Reading Workshop* (Ward Lock).

Pre-reading booklets

These booklets accompany most of the basic reading schemes, and some have been published independently:

Going Places in Reading Readiness, Reading Skill Text Series (Charles E. Merrill).

A.E. Tansley and R.H. Nicholls, *Getting Ready,* Early to Read Series (E.J. Arnold).

Derek and Lucy Thackray, *Steps to Reading,* Books 1 and 2 (George Philip Alexander).

C. Carver, *Oxford Junior Workbooks* 1 and 2 (OUP).

Buy two copies of the selected booklets so that each page can be mounted on cardboard. Sort the cards into categories: Visual Discrimination, Auditory Discrimination, Left-to-right Eye Movement, etc. This is a cheap way of obtaining a large quantity of material.

Visual, Tactile and Form Perception

The activities that can be incorporated in a pre-reading programme are many and varied. While simple discrimination activities such as matching pictures, colours and geometric shapes, are suitable beginning activities, they do not help the child in the complex task of discriminating between words (sentences, letters) in books. The child must go on to more difficult discrimination exercises with letters and combinations of letters, and reversals. 'Visual exploration, visual scanning and visual perception of the symbol system used in print are first-year learning tasks of major importance which have been neglected because they are difficult to observe and record.'[4]

It is impossible to list all the resources that could be included to develop visual discrimination, memory and sequencing, tactile and form perception, so a selection has been made. Refer to the Further Reading list headed Various Aspects. In addition, the following references and materials are useful:

A.E. Tansley, *Reading and Remedial Reading* (Routledge and Kegan Paul).

E. Goodacre, *Children and Learning to Read* (Routledge and Kegan Paul).

S. Haskell and M. Paull, *Training in Basic Cognitive Skills* (ESA).
Training in Basic Motor Skills (ESA).

Marianne Frostig and David Horne, *Frostig Programme for the Development of Visual Perception* (NFER).

J. Jackson and J. Reeve, *Look* — Workbooks, Stencils, Teachers' handbook (Macmillan).

Educational Toys and Games:

ESA Equipment — Look and Find the Story; Graded Pictures.

Galt Games — Remember, Remember; Spot the Set.

E.J. Arnold — Snappy Lotto; Picture Dominoes; Which Go Together?; What Do they Eat?

Philograph — Pictures and Shape Sorting Cards; Hereward Observation Test Matching Tablets: Shape Analysis Matching Cards.

Kiddicraft, Toltoy, Lego, Tinker, Dusyma, Rigby, Playskool — Construction sets, blocks, toys, beads and pattern making equipment. (Visual and motor development.)

Auditory Perception

See references and resources listed under Further Reading: Various Aspects, and the following:

Sound Stories; Sounds the Same; Sound Absurdities; Listen Here (LDA).

James O. Smith, *Peabody Articulation Cards* (NFER).

Sound Order Sense: A Developmental Programme in Auditory Perception (Follett Educational).

Listening to Sounds (E.J. Arnold).

Pictures for Sounds (ESA).

Look I'm Reading (ESA).

New Chelsea Pictorial Alphabet, (Philograph).

The literature programme should include story-telling by the teacher, mainly for enjoyment, but also for the development of listening skill, language and story sense.

When a programme of auditory discrimination activities has been undertaken by a child, the *Wepman Test* can be administered. (J.M. Wepman, *Auditory Discrimination Test,* NFER). No visual ability is needed for this test. It measures the ability to hear accurately. 'A pupil who scores low on this test obviously won't be able to read through phonics until this ability is greatly strengthened. If his visual discrimination is high then the teacher should use 'look-say' methods to increase reading ability, while at the same time gradually improving his auditory skills'.[5]

Stimulating the Desire to Read

Researchers have found that children who read early come from families where:
☐ The parents and siblings have a high regard for reading.
☐ The children have been read to regularly at home, from an early age.
☐ Someone in the family took the time not only to read, but to answer questions about words and about reading.
   A child who does not have books in his home (suitable books, which are read with him) will have missed experiences with bookish kinds of language, with concepts that are found only in books, and with picture exploration, and he will lack practice in co-ordinating language and visual perception in a way that facilitates progress with reading after entry into school.[6]

Interest in Books
☐ Read daily from *picture-story books* for enjoyment. Encourage individual perusal of books, and discussion of illustrations.
☐ Explain to children what you are doing as you use *informational books* so that they see various purposes in using books.
☐ Display simple story books (e.g. *Bruna Books,* Methuen) attractively and encourage children to 'read' them.
☐ Make *'experience' books* concerning the activities of the *whole class* (e.g. excursions, classroom pet) using their language and ideas, and encourage them to 'read' this material.
☐ Make *individual 'experience' books* for each child, using his sentences. Share this important reading experience with him in the most profitable ways so that reading becomes a meaningful personal experience.
N.B. Captions in home-made books should reinforce

directional rules, i.e. obviously the sentence will be written from left-to-right, and it will assist the child if it starts at the top left corner of the left page, then the top left corner of the right page, creating a correct 'position habit' as he turns each page.

☐ *Simple caption books* are an excellent introduction to reading. The way the child attacks such books should be noted by the teacher. Children with a great deal of pre-school experience with books will probably read many of these quite early in the year.

Read it Yourself Series (Methuen).

PM Instant Readers (Methuen).

A Lot of Things (Oliver and Boyd).

Methuen Caption Series (Methuen).

First Words Series (Macmillan).

This is my Colour/This is my Shape (George Philip Alexander).

Super Butch Books: Set 2 (Cassell).

Do You Know Words (Methuen).

Terraced House Books (Methuen).

This is the Way I Go (Longman).

Interest in Print

Does the child know that print tells the story? Or does he think when you read to him that you are telling a story about the pictures? He must learn that print conveys a message, and that his oral speech can be recorded in print. The best way to do this is to use print in meaningful situations, starting with his own name if he has not learnt it before attending school. Informal activities draw children's attention to words and their function:

☐ *Labelling* — specimens on the nature table; children's constructions; art and craft.

☐ *Notices, directions, reports, memoranda, charts, lists* — related to daily activities, excursions and experiments.

☐ *Wall stories and poems.*

☐ *Experience books* (see above).

Further Reading

Marie M. Clay, *Reading: The Patterning of Complex Behaviour* (Heinemann Educational).

Nora Goddard, *Literacy: Language-Experience Approaches* (Macmillan).

D. Lee and R.V. Allen, *Learning to Read through Experience* (Appleton Century Crofts).

V. Southgate and G.R. Roberts, *Reading — Which Approach?* (Hodder and Stoughton).

B. Thompson, *Learning to Read* (Sidgwick and Jackson).

Language Development

When we try to provide experiences that will compensate for poor language backgrounds we must go beyond the usual bounds of spontaneous learning in a free play situation or group learning from one teacher. The child's spontaneous wish to communicate about something which interests him at one particular moment should have priority, and he must have adults who will talk with him in simple, varied and grammatical language. We should arrange for language-producing activities — activities where adult and child must communicate in order to co-operate . . . Scheduled periods of close interaction with a familiar adult are needed and activities should stimulate a flow of ideas from the child and personal responses from the helper or teacher. [7]

An environment rich in opportunities for communication and an atmosphere encouraging language development are essential. Bear in mind Clay's questions as the child participates in various interesting play activities:

Does the play activity bring the child into conversational exchange with a mature language model? What opportunities are there for one-to-one conversational exchanges with an adult who understands the child's frame of reference and so shapes up the word and grammar skills of a particular individual? [8]

The teacher's success or failure in one-to-one contact will depend greatly on the number of children in the class.

The language aspects of all activities should be exploited. For example, in perceptual training activities, when a child has sorted and classified objects, or placed picture cards in sequence, he should have the opportunity to discuss the activity: to explain the categorization, or to tell the story sequence. If this is omitted, part of the educational value of the activity is lost.

To an observant teacher the child's language is the link with his first reading matter. (See: Stimulating the Desire to Read p.15).

Picture books (i.e. without texts) can be used to encourage language. Some of the following depict factual sequences, and others are imaginative, encouraging creative responses:

'Language in Action Resource Books — Pre-literacy level', Joyce Morris *(Macmillan Language Project)*

Stories Without Words (Nelson).

Peabody Language Development Kit (NFER).

Board Books (The Bodley Head).

Dominoes Picture Books (Oliver and Boyd).

Picture Reading (Ladybird Series 721, Wills and Hepworth).

A Story to Tell; Another Story to Tell, Dick Bruna (Methuen).

A Boy, A Dog and A Frog, M. Mayer (Collins).

Johnny's Bad Day, Ardizzone (The Bodley head).

One to Eleven, Yutaka Sugita (Evans).

Picture Stories, Rodney Pepper (Picture Puffins).

Look What I Can Do, Jose Aruego (Hamish Hamilton).

The Circus, Brian Wildsmith (OUP).

The Chicken and the Egg, The Apple and the Butterfly, etc. I. and E. Mari (A. & C. Black).

Changes, Changes, Pat Hutchins (Picture Puffin).

See also *Individualised Reading: Comparative Lists of Selected Books for Young Readers,* Stage O, Cliff Moon (Centre for the Teaching of Reading, University of Reading).

books is, perhaps, the most valuable, some work with small groups of children using *large discussion pictures* can be helpful.

The literature programme (stories, poetry, rhymes) increases the child's vocabulary and stimulates him to talk, re-tell, chant rhymes, to express himself creatively, perhaps in painting, and to talk about his creation.

Picture sequences encourage language and left-to-right orientation: e.g. Audio-visual education charts (See: Visual Perception p.8); Pre-reading work books — basic reading schemes (See Further Reading: Various Aspects p.12).

Further Reading

See Further Reading: Various Aspects, p.12, for useful references and resources, also the following:

Nora Goddard, *Literacy: Language-Experience Approaches* (Macmillan).

Alice Yardley, *Exploration and Language* (Evans).

Joan Dean, *Reading, Writing and Talking* (A. & C. Black).

Sensory-motor Development

Hand-Eye Motor Co-ordination

The following games, activities and toys are valuable for the development of co-ordination:

Ludo, Snakes and Ladders, Marbles, Dot-to-dot, Pick-up-sticks, Meccano and other construction toys.

Art and craft activities using scissors, paste, brushes, etc.; knitting, sewing, weaving, sawing, hammering, etc.

Activities to Promote Left-to-Right Eye Movement

Some pre-reading and pre-writing workbooks and materials include tracing and copying exercises which assist left-to-right orientation and eye-hand co-ordination, e.g.

Eye-Hand Integration Exercises (LDA).

A.E. Tansley and R.H. Nicholls, *Getting Ready*, Early to Read, First Book (E.J. Arnold).

S. Haskell and M. Paull, *Training in Basic Motor Skills* (ESA).
Training in Basic Cognitive Skills (ESA).

Language in Action: Pre-literacy Level booklets, Joyce Morris (Macmillan) encourage left-to-right orientation, as well as book-handling and language skills.

It is not self-evident to a child that left to right movement along a line, through a book, and across a word are related. And telling him that they are will not be sufficient. It is only through working with print, writing his own stories, reading and discovering things about printed texts, that he slowly consolidates the total network of relationships.[9]

Further Reading

C. McCharney and N.C. Kephart, *Motoric Aids to Perceptual Training* (Charles E. Merrill).

Marianne Frostig, *Move-Grow-Learn Program* (NFER).

A.E. Tansley, *Reading and Remedial Reading* (Routledge and Kegan Paul).

M. and J.B. Ebersole, N.C. Kephart, *Steps to Achievement for the Slow Learner* (Charles E. Merrill).

D.H. Radler and N.C. Kephart, *Success through Play* (Harper and Row).

Marianne Frostig, *Movement Education Theory and Practice* (NFER).

A.S. Eispenschade and H.M. Eckert, *Motor Development* (Charles E. Merrill).

Observation of Readiness

For some children, especially those who have had extensive nursery-school experience, a programme of pre-reading activities, conducted for several months, can be a waste of time. (It is expected that these children would be a minority group.) The child who, in Entry Screening Tests, indicates that he can distinguish beginning, rhyming, and ending sounds in words, is probably ready to learn phonics. Extended sessions of simple listening games have value, for this child, only as a social activity. Similarly, the child who performs well on complex visual perception tasks, and shows maturity in other areas as well, is probably ready to learn initial reading. The child who is already reading will need a sequential programme of reading.

The teacher's problem is an organizational one — how to provide for many different levels of maturity in reading readiness. Those who are advanced should be able to select from many different ongoing general activities, and they should be able to progress with reading instead of participating in specialized pre-reading activities.

The teacher who gives every child pre-reading training may well be doing many children a grave disservice because they don't need it.

The only definite evidence that a child is ready to read is when print begins to make sense to him. So the child should be *encouraged* to read and have a learning environment where interesting books are freely and easily available and where there is no stigma attached to being unable to read.[10]

Marie Clay believes that often when a child seems immature, 'waiting for readiness' is not the best solution:

Waiting for 'readiness' will not organise early reading behaviour in a way that provides a good foundation for later progress.[11]

There is a strong case for training the immature child in the task of printed language and for giving him supplementary tuition of a more controlled, detailed and structured kind in his area of weakness.[12]

The key to a successful programme is observation of individuals.

Having a 'good programme' for a large group and not watching individuals learn will result in the survival of the fittest. Those who can, will learn; those who cannot, will become confused or develop false concepts and handicapping strategies. [13]

Teachers are accused of paying 'lip-service' to the ideal of individual learning and development, but it is impossible for teachers of new entrants to put ideals into practice while they work with large classes.

Obviously, *time* must be available for effective individual observation, recording, evaluation and action. Classes must be smaller (perhaps 20 in a class, which is nearer to the nursery-school class size) for successful initial teaching. This in turn is a programme for prevention of failure, and would decrease the need for later remedial teaching which is costly in both human and financial terms.

A Stable Environment

It is most important that the child has a secure and predictable environment during the first year so that teacher observation and child progress are uninterrupted.

Poor attendance means haphazard contact with various skills, and little reinforcement. This can increase the child's uncertainty and confusion, indicating a poor start to learning reading. Definite steps need to be taken to bridge gaps.

Early Remedial Action

In a complex learning task like learning to read there is a danger that a child will learn wrong associations at any time in the learning sequence, and will become confused. Marie Clay regards failure in the first year as a vital clue to the child's reading future, and she deplores the fact that many children are not given remedial help until they are eight. Meanwhile they have had three years of failure, frustration, reinforcement of inefficient reading behaviour and practice of wrong responses. After one year a diagnostic survey should be made, Clay suggests, then:

A flexible and experienced teacher, well versed in individualized-teaching techniques, and especially qualified in a wide variety of

approaches to reading instruction, must be available for intensive and sustained re-teaching of low progress children in their second year at school on the basis of the results of this diagnostic survey.[14]

One important point to note in diagnosing readiness is that if a child is not learning to read, this does not necessarily mean he is not ready to read.

He may not be ready for the approach his teacher is using; he may be perfectly ready for a different approach.[15]

D. Communicating Meaning: Decoding

Do you know the terms *phoneme* and *grapheme*? What does a child understand when you talk about a 'sound' and a 'letter'? How confusing is it for him? How can you help?

Breaking the code of the written language involves a problem-solving operation just as mathematical learning does but first of all a child must understand what a code is.

Many things which adults take for granted are puzzling for children. Even with the greatest care, we are bound sometimes to drop into the habitual use of words and concepts which are beyond the child's present understanding. But, as Piaget has shown, the child is unaware of his inability to comprehend. He believes he can understand and he tries to do so by 'syncretistic' approximations to our meaning.

In other words, the child tries to guess what we mean when we use unfamiliar ideas. He develops hunches and tries them out to see if they work. By a process of intellectual trial and error he comes closer and closer to the generally accepted concept.

Reading is no exception to this rule. What the grown-ups mean by 'reading', 'writing', 'word', 'letter', 'sound', etc., all have to be puzzled out through feedback from the experience of trying to guess their meaning. But, curiously, educators seldom recognize that learning to read constitutes a set of problems to be solved by the child, although this state of affairs is generally recognized in relation to mathematics. Perhaps literacy seems to adults to be merely a simple extension of oral language, whereas numeracy appears to be a special, separate subject to be more deliberately learned.

The truth is that literacy learning, with its attendant under-standing of the linguistic concepts involved, is just as much a problem-solving operation as mathematical learning.

One similarity between mathematics and literacy learning is that both involve codes. What is more instructive for teachers of reading is to consider that in both cases it is a *double* code. In maths we use words like 'one', 'two', 'half', 'twice', etc., which themselves constitute an abstract code for more concrete operations. This is the primary code.

Then we have to relate this to a secondary written code with symbols such as '1', '2', '$\frac{1}{2}$', '2 x', etc. Recognition of such steps has revolutionized primary maths in recent years by giving priority to children's understanding of mathematical concepts instead of the rote learning of written formulae.

The same needs to be done in primary reading. All our spoken language is a primary code abstracted from the real world which our words and ideas only represent. Written language is a secondary code of visual symbols signifying the primary code of speech. In the development of literacy skills, priority should be given to providing children with this understanding of the basic linguistic concepts and principles from which reading and writing develop.

Research (see *Further Reading*) shows quite clearly that normal five-year-olds do not understand the basic concept of symbolization either in the special area of maths or in language in general. They have no notion of a code in which one thing can represent something else. Therefore, the child has a much more difficult task than simply learning to decode writing to speech or encode speech into written symbols. He has to solve the problem of *what is a code?* and *what are all these aspects of the code the adults talk about as if they were self-evident?* (e.g. 'word', 'sound', 'letter', etc.). He understands neither the purpose nor the mechanism of coding.

Many writers have focussed on ways of teaching the *purpose* of reading. Here our concern is more with helping children to understand and use its *mechanism*. But these two aspects of coding are inextricably linked. The first fundamental fact the child needs to understand about coding is its purpose; i.e. to symbolize meaning.

Written language is a code for communicating the concepts

of spoken language. Therefore, the first examples of coding which we present to beginners must demonstrate clearly and consistently the essential purpose of writing language to communicate meaning.

Just imagine what it would be like if someone said to you, 'this + stands for a *blahbark*' i.e. the written code symbol '+' represents the spoken code symbol 'blahbark'. This is what premature phonics teaching sounds like to the young beginner. Even worse is the phonics instruction: '+' says *blahbark*. When *we ourselves* are faced with the nonsense task of associating two meaningless code symbols we realize how such inept methods make the problems of learning to read even more difficult for the child to solve then they need to be.

Obviously, the child must understand the primary code of speech *first* if he is going to associate its symbols with the secondary code of writing.

The basic unit of the primary code of spoken English is the *phoneme*. The more popular term is 'sound' — but this is an ambiguous word, and can refer even to auditory stimuli which have nothing to do with speech. A *phoneme* is more precisely defined — a unit of speech sound within a word which affects the meaning of the utterance. English has approximately 40 phonemes (approximately, because of dialect differences and the differences of opinion among linguists). All the vast vocabulary of our language consists of permutations of these few phonemes.

Research quite clearly shows that children can easily discriminate auditorily between single words which vary by only one phoneme, but probably not on the basis of that unit. They are not aware of and do not understand that they are using a phonemic code.

To understand the mechanism of the written code, children must first learn this phonemic code system. A variety of interesting activities must be provided to help children develop the concept of phoneme and to be able to hear these sound units in spoken words and phrases. They need to know how many phonemes a word has, what phoneme it begins with, ends with, etc. Time spent in using auditory discrimination apparatus must not be begrudged.

Another lesson which reading teachers can learn from

modern mathematics teaching is to 'make haste slowly' — to make quite certain that the child *understands* what he is doing and why.

But we do not need to wait until the child knows all the 40 phonemes of English in this way. So long as he thoroughly understands the concept of phoneme and can juggle with phonemes readily, then he is ready to learn the written code for phonemes.

A phoneme is represented in our alphabetic system by a *grapheme*. We cannot say 'letter' because sometimes a phoneme is written by more than one letter, e.g. *oo* in m*oo*n, or *ough* in b*ough*. We cannot say that the graphemes are equal to the 26 letters of our alphabet. The 44 phonemes of the spoken code of English are represented in our written code by hundreds of different graphemes.

Although there are hundreds of them, they contain many regularities of correspondence with phonemes. Only a minority are idiosyncratic. All must be learned eventually, whether we begin with all of them as in t.o. (traditional orthography) or postpone this total array until after an initial period with a regular code of graphemes for phonemes such as i.t.a.

Probably i.t.a. owes its success less to the simpler operation of learning these regular connections between i.t.a. graphemes and English phonemes than is generally supposed. It may be the case that i.t.a. has succeeded almost accidentally in a less direct manner. Its regularity has clarified for teachers as well as children the concepts of (1) phoneme and (2) the coding function of written language in general.

Further Reading

J.A. Downing, 'How Children Think About Reading', *The Reading Teacher,* Vol. 23 No. 3, pp 217-30.

J.F. Reid, 'Learning to Think About Reading', *Educational Research,* Vol. 9 No. 56, pp 56-62.

M.D. Vernon, *Backwardness in Reading* (CUP).

3   The Initial Teaching of Reading

How Children Learn to Read

Learning to read involves the almost simultaneous processing of the ideas presented by written materials, the interpretation of sentence patterns expressing these ideas and a recognition of the words within the sentences. It is a highly complex cognitive task.

The various abilities involved in learning to read are intelligence, language facility, visual abilities, auditory abilities, physical factors, environmental influences and emotional factors. Goodman has termed reading 'a psycholinguistic guessing game'.

In our present state of knowledge there is no known correct or perfect way to approach the teaching of reading. Methods which are highly successful with teacher A and children X may not work at all for teacher B with children Y or with children X. This is because the process of learning to read is such a complex mixture of individual abilities, skills and personality traits . . . The teacher must have a thorough knowledge of the children as individuals and an understanding not only of the techniques involved in various teaching methods, but also of the advantages and disadvantages involved. [1]

Teachers trying to evaluate the specific and relative values of various approaches will find *Reading — Which Approach?* by Vera Southgate and G.R. Roberts (Hodder and Stoughton, 1970) very helpful. They suggest that the teacher must first decide her role. Is she a 'teacher-leader', believing in systematic and progressive planning of instruction and learning, or a 'teacher-counsellor', believing in incidental learning within an appropriate school environment? The former sees her role in the foreground as an initiator, a leader; the latter prefers to be in the background as a guide.

Having decided which set of beliefs she embraces, each teacher can set about choosing the most suitable approach and materials for herself and her children, using the authors' suggested criteria.

They examine three 'look-and-say' approaches, three phonic approaches, and three examples of approaches that introduce different media (Words in Colour, Colour Story Reading, i.t.a.). Certain schemes are selected for detailed assessment.

An extensive study was undertaken in the United States by Dr Jeanne Chall (published in *Learning to Read: The Great Debate,* McGraw Hill, 1967). She reviewed all the research evidence on how to begin the teaching of reading, and she consulted teachers and experts of all kinds. She observed teachers at work in 300 classrooms in the United States and the United Kingdom and reviewed texts of the most popular reading schemes (twenty-two programmes in all).

Chall would seem to have gathered enough evidence to support her claims that:

- ☐ Children will respond equally well to the challenge of both phonic methods and 'look-and-say' approaches;
- ☐ Methods giving emphasis to 'code-cracking' (i.e. phonic methods), consistently proved to be equal or superior to those that were strongly 'sight' based;
- ☐ 'Look-and-say' methods and materials are not intrinsically more interesting to the child than linguistic and phonic methods and materials;
- ☐ The teacher's attitudes and beliefs are important — what teachers themselves find interesting they can and will make interesting for children;
- ☐ The teacher's treatment of the method (whichever method she chooses), is the crucial factor in the pupil's learning to read.

As children work through the pre-reading programme they reveal different needs, limitations and abilities. Teachers need to select appropriate methods of teaching initial reading to meet these various individual needs. Therefore, it is important that teachers understand and are able to use several methods.

Further Reading

J. Chall, *Learning to Read: The Great Debate* (McGraw Hill).
D. Moyle, *The Teaching of Reading,* (Ward Lock Educational 4th edn).
V. Southgate and G. R. Roberts, *Reading: Which Approach?* (Hodder and
    Stoughton).
E. Goodacre, *Children and Learning to Read* (Routledge and Kegan Paul).

(1) Summary of Approaches

A. Synthetic Methods

1. Phonic Approaches

These methods aim to teach the learner word attack skills
from the beginning so that he can become independent as
soon as possible in both reading and writing.

Children learn sounds and letters, and analyse and
synthesize words.

Most phonic-based programmes restrict vocabulary in order
to establish regularity of sound-symbol relationships.

(a) J.C. Daniels and H. Diack believe that 'look-and-say'
approaches are partly responsible for the large number of
children failing to master the reading process. They developed
the *Royal Road Readers* — a sequential phonic reading
scheme.

Further Reading

J.C. Daniels and H. Diack, *Progress in Reading in the Infant School*
    (Nottingham Institute of Education University of Nottingham).
H. Diack, *In Spite of the Alphabet* (Chatto and Windus).
R. Flesch, *Why Johnny Can't Read* (Harper and Row).

(b) Professor D.H. Stott's *Programmed Reading Kit* is more
suitable for remedial work with older failing readers than for
teaching initial reading to infants as it is fairly steeply graded.

Further Reading

D.H. Stott, *Programmed Reading Kit Manual* (Holmes McDougall).
D.H. Stott, *Roads to Literacy* (Holmes McDougall).

(c) *New orthographies and systems.* There are thousands of irregularities in the English language, e.g. the long 'i' sound; eye, high, I, might, height, hide, cry, by, buy, isle, aisle.

Attempts have been made to regularize the English language for the purposes of teaching intitial reading:

☐ Dr Caleb Gattegno's *Words in Colour* — each sound is represented by a colour (47 different colours).

☐ Sir James Pitman's *Initial Teaching Alphabet* (i.t.a.) is an alphabet of 44 characters, each sound being represented by one symbol.

☐ Kenneth Jones' *Colour Story Reading* is a modified colour system. Three colours and three background shapes are used to aid identification of sounds.

Further Reading

C. Gattegno, *Words in Colour* (Educational Explorers Ltd.).
J.A. Downing, *Evaluating the Initial Teaching Alphabet* (Cassell).
J.K. Jones, *Colour Story Reading* (Nelson).

2. Linguistic Programmes

These are similar to phonic programmes. Firstly, the alphabet is learnt as a code. Then the programme concentrates on regularly-spelled whole words which are to be read as such. If they are not immediately recognized, the code is applied to them. There is an element of self-discovery in linguistic programmes that is less apparent in phonics programmes. Oral language provides the child with context clues to reading.

Two schemes which combine linguistic with language-experience approaches are:

Reading 360 (Ginn)
Language in Action (Macmillan).

Further Reading

C.C. Fries, *Linguistics and Reading* (Holt, Rinehart and Winston).

B. Analytic Methods ('Look-and-say', Recognition or 'Whole' Approaches)

These methods stress reading for *meaning* from the beginning using whole words and/or sentences to teach initial reading.

Systematic instruction in phonics begins after the learner has acquired a 'sight vocabulary'.

These methods are used with many basic reading schemes currently in use, e.g. *Time for Reading* (Ginn).

These schemes feature 'controlled vocabulary' to assist recognition.

1. Sentence Method

Sentences are introduced from either the basic reader or from the children's experiences.

Gradually words are isolated from the sentences and children recognize them.

When most of the vocabulary is known the first reader is introduced and the child reads it without further teaching.

Phonics is taught and children's ability to attack words independently is developed.

2. Word Method

This method is similar to the sentence method, but words are taught first and then combined to form sentences.

Further Reading
F.J. Schonell and E.J. Goodacre, *The Psychology and Teaching of Reading* (Oliver & Boyd, 5th edn.).

C. The Learner-Centred Trend or the Language-Experience Approach

The chief aim is the development of the learner.

Reading is a response to the environment. The child is placed in a situation rich in potential experiences and attractive books, and is stimulated to use language.

He soon seeks a permanent record of experiences that are real and vital to him.

At first the teacher writes for him, and later he writes for himself. This is his first reading material.

Reading is seen as an integral part of total language development — listening, speaking, reading and writing. Strong links between reading and writing from the beginning encourage the development of written expression as well as reading skills.

Materials such as *Breakthrough to Literacy* (Longman) cater not only for widely differing child needs, but also help in overcoming the teacher's problem of preparation of materials.

Further Reading

M.A. Hall, *Teaching Reading as a Language Experience* (Charles E. Merrill).

Roma Gans, *Guiding Children's Reading through Experiences* (Teachers College, Columbia University).

D. Lee and R.V. Allen, *Learning to Read through Experience* (Appleton Century Crofts).

N. Goddard, *Literacy: Language Experience Approaches* (The Language Project, Macmillan).

D. Individualized Reading Approaches

The needs of the learner are of paramount importance.

The learner is surrounded by a wide variety of reading material at many levels of difficulty and in many areas of interest. Anything in print is legitimate reading matter.

Self-selection of material for reading is encouraged.

The learner is assisted as far as possible to help himself and to become responsible for his own education.

Help is given by the teacher 'as needed' rather than on a planned structured basis.

These approaches are suggested by Goodman, Holt, Kohl and other advocates of 'alternative' education.

Further Reading

Herbert Kohl, *Reading, How to* (Penguin).

Leland Jacobs, *Individualizing Reading Practices* (Teachers College, Columbia University).

George Pappas, *Reading in the Primary School* (Macmillan).

L.A. Harris and C.B. Smith, *Individualizing Reading Instruction* (Holt, Rinehart and Winston).

John Holt, *How Children Fail* (Penguin).

E. Multi-Sensory Reinforcement

Multi-sensory reinforcement is an aid to the teaching of reading or spelling, and can be used with any method of teaching. It is a means of consolidating visual and auditory impressions (or words, letters or figures).

Multi-sensory activities are not new. In the 1920s Grace Fernald used kinaesthetic techniques in teaching retarded children to read. (Grace Fernald, *Remedial Techniques in Basic School Subjects,* McGraw Hill).

Here is a suggestion for using multi-sensory reinforcement. In the teaching of initial reading by sentence method, the sentence to be taught, either from the child's experience:

'Our rabbit likes to eat carrots.'

or from the first reader in a basic scheme:

'Timothy is playing with his trains.'

(From 'The Cherry Family', *Time for Reading* Ginn), may be presented in the following way:

☐ The teacher prints the sentence on the blackboard while the children watch. She describes the formation of the letters and words as she prints.

☐ The teacher and the children read the sentence, individually and together.

☐ The teacher writes the sentence again and the children trace it in the air, on their arm, or on the floor.

☐ The teacher prints the sentence on an indicator card and adds an illustration. She prints the sentence on another card without illustration (for flashcard games and matching activities).

☐ Isolation of a word. The teacher tells the children that she is going to rub out a word, e.g. 'with' (or 'his' or 'playing'). She deletes it from one sentence and asks a child to point to it in the other sentence. The children can trace it in the air, on the floor, etc, as the teacher writes it. (The teacher is gradually building up a sight vocabulary of useful words for later reading and writing activities).

☐ Multi-sensory treatment of word or sentence — use any one of the following techniques:

    — The word or sentence is printed on paper by the teacher. The child traces with his forefinger, then with pencil or crayon, and illustrates.

— The word or sentence is printed on paper by the teacher. The child traces with his forefinger, then with paste brush, and attaches sawdust, paper snippets, sand, cottonwool, string, wool, or confetti. When this is dry he traces with his finger again, reading the word or sentence.

— The word is printed on paper by the teacher. The child makes 'snakes' with clay, dough or plasticine, and makes the word over the teacher's copy.

— The sentence is presented on paper by the teacher. The child cuts it up into words, then remakes the sentence and pastes it on paper, and illustrates it.

☐ If the sentence is intended as part of the child's first reader, the teacher prints it into his individual experience book.

N.B. — Take care that these activities (especially pasting exercises) do not degenerate into 'busy-work', filling in time without much benefit being gained.

Difficult abstract words such as 'was' and 'there' can be treated in this manner, not only at the initial reading stage, but at any time in the primary school.

Multi-sensory reinforcement is useful in teaching phonics for initial reading, or as an attack skill to be mastered after a 'look-and-say' initial approach.

It is clear that writing activities closely related to reading are of great value in promoting progress in reading.[2]

F. The Reading Programme: First Year

It is likely that the initial teaching of reading will be under-taken in the first year for many of the new entrants. Here is a summary of several important considerations stressed in regard to the pre-reading programme and applicable to the early reading programme:

☐ If *individual teaching* is to be undertaken, *small classes* are necessary.

☐ *Observation, recording and evaluation,* important pre-liminaries to diagnostic teaching, should be carried out again this is possible only in small classes.

☐ *A stable environment* is necessary for observation and positive reinforcement.

☐ *Early success is vital.* There is research evidence to suggest that reading behaviour becomes organized into a complex system of functioning during the first two years of instruction, in a way that sets the pattern for subsequent gains in skill. If the system functions efficiently the child reads fluently without much error and adds to his skill with every exposure to this task. If the system functions inefficiently the child establishes habits of inefficient processing of cues with every extra reading lesson he has.[3]

☐ *Remedial action must not be deferred.* Remedial efforts will be most economical when applied close to the point where the faulty learning begins, after one year of instruction.[4]

Unquestionably the greatest single cause of failure (in learning to read) remains the distressingly high pupil-to-staff ratio which means that in subjects like reading the teacher is often doing little more than managing.[5]

(2) Several Approaches Outlined[6]

A. An Argument in Support of a Language — Experience Approach to the Teaching of Reading

For so long, five-year-olds have been introduced to reading by means of Basic Readers which are totally foreign to the child's experience of life. In both content, and language, the commonly used sequential reading schemes are inappropriate for use with the majority of children who enter the preparatory classes of our primary schools. All of the well known series are centred around a middle-class, nuclear family of Mother, Father, one boy, one girl, one baby of no apparent sex, one dog and one cat, who all live together in a single-storey, detached house, surrounded by a well kept garden. Mother stays at home with baby, Father goes to work each morning in his neatly pressed suit, armed with hat and briefcase, and returns promptly, and soberly, before dinner each evening. The baby is never sick, the children never fight, the parents never disagree, and all live together in fairy tale happiness. These unbelievable characters speak to each other in a succession of commands, interspread with innumerable exclamations. '*Oh! Oh! Come! Come! See here!*'

How meaningful is this to most contemporary children?

> Reading has the most meaning to a child when the materials being read are expressed in his language and are rooted in his experiences. [7]

When the reading material is designed by an adult author, he calls on his own background of experience to determine the content and the language. If this background of experience is not shared by the reader, then problems of misunderstanding or lack of understanding may occur.

When the reading material uses the same background of experiences as that of the reader, then no conflict occurs, and the reading material is understood by the reader.

> Reading is a language-based process which is used for the transmission of meaning through the interpretation of printed symbols. The complex process of reading includes the decoding of print, the association of meaning with the printed code, and the reaction of the reader as he associates an author's meaning with his previous experience. [8]

The most meaningful words a child can read are those within his spoken vocabulary, and it is these words, arising from his verbalization of direct experiences, which are taken and made into reading material in the Language-Experience Approach to Reading.

> The research and opinion would suggest that an instructional programme designed to develop an understanding of the relationship between the child's familiar spoken system of communication and written language would facilitate his ability to comprehend written material. [9]

The Language-Experience Approach to Reading sees reading as one aspect of language — interrelated and interdependent. Listening, speaking, reading and writing are all equally important aspects of language.

Language can be seen as oral and written, and as expressive and receptive.

The oral areas are speaking and listening. The written areas are writing and reading. Expression is conveyed through speaking and writing, and messages are received through listening and reading. It is because of the interrelation and interdependence of the four areas of language that the language experience approach does not attempt to isolate reading from the spoken language of children, nor does it treat reading as separate from writing. The child writes those words that he hears and says, and the written words become his reading material.

Any new approach to reading must do all the things that earlier successful approaches did — only more so, and more effectively. The primary goal of reading instruction is to develop children's ability to use reading as a medium of communication. It must:

☐ Build up children's reading vocabularies;
☐ Establish effective means of word attack;
☐ Develop comprehension ability;
☐ Promote a favourable attitude toward, and permanent interest in reading.

Applegate[10] identifies the goals of the language arts as follows:

☐ To use words responsibly;
☐ To think clearly;
☐ To listen imaginatively;
☐ To speak effectively;
☐ To read thoughtfully;
☐ To write creatively;
☐ To use mechanics powerfully;
☐ To regard good English respectfully;
☐ To acquaint children with the best in literature.

A successful language-experience approach teaches both reading and language arts skills in situations which necessitate meaningful communication.

The Learning Environment

Apart from the teacher, who is the most important single influence on learning in any given classroom, the classroom environment is of paramount importance, and must include an air of acceptance as well as providing stimuli for creativity.

If the child's spoken language is to provide the material for his reading, then two conditions are absolutely essential. The child must be accepted as he is — with all his charm, with all his problems; and in particular, the stage of development he has reached must be accepted without question.

He must feel comfortable and free to use the language that is his own.[11] The other condition necessary for the successful launching of a language experience approach is a stimulating environment, one that provides freedom to explore, and a challenge to investigate. If these two conditions are provided, oral language will flourish, and it is this spoken form of language that is the prerequisite for reading. In order to read meaningfully, the child must be able to speak fluently, and in order to do this he must have experiences to talk about as well as the language in which to communicate, or restructure experience.

Having provided an accepting, stimulating environment which encourages flow of language, the teacher is ready to consider the initial acquisition of literacy. Her first consideration will be the children. How ready are they to tackle the complex process of reading? Previously, children were subjected to a graded series of pre-reading exercises, regardless of whether these were appropriate or not, and regardless of whether the child saw these exercises as part of reading. Visual discrimination exercises used geometric shapes and colour, but did not discriminate between letters and words — skills needed in reading. Research has shown that distinguishing similarities and differences between letters and between words is directly related to the perceptual tasks involved in reading whereas discriminating between pictures in a row, or discriminating between geometric shapes is not the same visual task as that required in reading.[12] Pre-reading instruction in visual discrimination, letter names, auditory discrimination, left-to-right progression, language development, and interest in reading can all be approached from a language experience framework. The important task in this pre-reading stage is for the teacher to really get to know her children and their stage of readiness. She must ask herself;

☐ Which children come from homes where reading occurs, and which do not?

☐ Which children know what books are?

□ Which children have had stories read to them at home?
□ Which children have any physical barriers to reading? Motor development may be slow, or impaired. Eyesight or hearing may be defective.
□ Which children talk fluently, and which do not?

By asking herself these and similar questions, the beginners' teacher can plan the learning environment most conducive to developing the skill of reading.

The Approach with a Class or Group

a) Introductory Session

□ *Initial stimulus* — common experience to promote oral language, both informally amongst children and, more directly, from individual to group.
□ *Activities resulting from stimulus* — e.g. model making with three-dimensional materials (waste paper), collage with scrap materials, modelling with clay, picture making, free dramatic play, etc.
□ *Formation of individual oral sentences* related to stimulus.
□ *Selection of one commonly accepted sentence,* to be written clearly on the board, and read by many children. Simple sentence analysis can be treated at this stage, introducing terms — sentence, word, space, full stop and capital letter.
□ *Picture making etc. based on the class sentence.* Teacher writes sentence on children's pictures. Some children trace over, or copy, the sentence.

b) Follow-up Activities

Use large sentence cards, both illustrated and plain. Once the children have isolated separate words, these are added as single word cards.

c) Extension

The sentence can be added to others on wall charts and in experience books, both class and individual, for further reading. Tactile experiences can be given using the sentence as a base for tracing, moulding words in rolled plasticene, covering with paste and sand, wool, confetti or soft spaghetti etc. Sentence analysis can be treated by reshuffling words of the sentence, and re-arranging to re-make the sentence.

Use of Published Books

Using the language-experience approach, it would not be necessary to include basic readers in the children's early reading material, but published books which met the criteria in terms of content and language would be readily available. As children come to recognize words in their interest sentences, they will find these words in published books.

There is no need to introduce vocabulary to the child before giving him the book, as he will already have encountered the words in his discussion of the topic, and in writing his interest sentences. The published book will consolidate the language he has been using orally.

Resource

Cliff Moon, *Individualised Reading: Comparative Lists of Selected Books for Young Readers* stages 1-3 (Centre for the Teaching of Reading, University of Reading).

Word Attack Skills

Any reading programme must teach children methods of attacking unfamiliar words quickly and independently.[13]

The skills needed for independence in word attack are configuration, phonics, stuctural analysis, context clues, and use of the dictionary. The teacher who is anxious to provide a systematic, definite programme in word attack skills, in addition to the other language-experience activities, can do so by forming flexible groups of children on the basis of need for a common skill. As the need changes, so will the group.

An awareness of phonics can be stimulated while interest-based sentences are being used. Some children will notice similarities are being used. Some children will notice similarities in word shapes and letter shapes, e.g. 'That shape there is in my name.' Whenever this occurs, the teacher takes the opportunity to isolate single letters by outlining them in colour, or writing them in isolation, and encouraging children to look for more similar letters and to listen for similar sounds. Lists of words with the same sound can be made, as well as books for each sound isolated.

As soon as children begin to isolate sounds and symbols,

these symbols can be written on a blending chart. As soon as there are a consonant and a vowel on the chart, the teacher can point to the two letters consecutively, asking the child to blend them together.

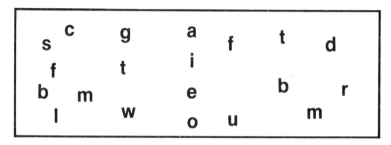

Evaluation

Informal evaluation can take place in everyday situations with spoken and written language. More formal evaluation can take the form of record keeping (e.g. anecdotal comments, check lists) and standardized tests.

It would be possible to evaluate children's learning to read in terms of those instructional goals previously outlined. A teacher would ask herself:

- ☐ Are the children increasing their ability to use reading as a medium of communication?
- ☐ Are reading vocabularies increasing?
- ☐ Are they developing favourable attitudes and genuine interest in reading?

How Does the Language-Experience Approach Operate in the Classroom?

With a Class, or Group of Children

- ☐ An interesting experience is shared by all the children. This experience promotes oral language between the children, and between the teacher and children, e.g. the children may all view a performance by visiting puppeteers.
- ☐ Many children compose sentences about the experience.
- ☐ One of these sentences is chosen by the children for the teacher to write on the blackboard. As she writes the sentence the teacher says the words and comments upon

the sentence structure. Terms such as capital letter and full stop are used, and attention is drawn to the spaces between words.
☐ Several children 'read' the sentence.
☐ The teacher again writes the sentence on the blackboard, this time sounding each word as it is written. She does not give the short sound made by the letter in isolation, but rather, she blends the sounds as they make up the spoken word.
☐ The sentence is read again by the children. The children then return to their tables to make puppets, model puppets in clay, paint pictures of the puppet show, act out a puppet play of their own, etc. Where children illustrate the puppet experience on paper, the teacher writes the class sentence beneath the child's drawing. These children are encouraged to trace over the written sentence, and perhaps try to copy the writing under the teacher's sample. After the lesson, the teacher makes two copies of the sentence — on an indicator card with an accompanying picture or sketch, and on a sentence card, with no illustration.

The indicator card is placed in a prominent position and both cards are used in subsequent lessons. When children start recognizing words, these too may be written on cards and used by the children in matching activities.

On following days the teacher prepares the sentences in advance on paper for the children to either trace over or copy.

Sentence activities may include:
☐ Matching sentence cards to indicator cards.
☐ Reading class experience books made up from children's experience sentences.
☐ Tracing over the sentence with crayons.
☐ Writing the sentence in a sand tray.
☐ Making the sentence with dough or plasticine.
☐ Covering the written sentence with wool, sawdust, etc.
☐ For those children who recognize words within the sentence, the sentence may be cut into words for the child to shuffle, and rearrange into the original sentence.

The Language-Experience Approach in an Individualized Programme

It can be argued that instruction as outlined above with a class or group cannot be a true language-experience approach for each child, as his own personal language is not forming the basis of a personalized reading programme. It is only in a truly individualized learning situation that this approach can operate at an individual level.

The same sequence of activities as outlined above may be worked through, i.e.

☐ Child gives sentence from some personal experience, or he draws in his personal reading book and asks the teacher to write the sentence for him.

☐ Teacher writes sentence for child in his own book.

☐ Child traces over the written sentence.

☐ Child writes underneath the written sentence.

☐ Child adds to the written sentence.

Group and Individualized Approaches

The child's reading programme should not be limited to his own sentences and experience books. Wall charts, and shared experience books should also be compiled, and reading should also be put to use around the room in the form of sentence labels, e.g.

Only three children may play with sand.
Can you sort the shells like this?
The rabbit is asleep. Please be quiet.

B. Reading: Linguistic Approaches

Modern studies in linguistics have led to the proposal of two widely differing approaches to the teaching of the early stages of reading. Lefevre (1964)[14] has proposed that all work upon word recognition should arise out of the material which the child speaks, reads or writes. Thus when the child is working upon word recognition skills he has already discovered the function of the word in the sentence and its meaning in that particular sentence.

It is suggested that by working in this way the uses to which reading can be put are never separated from the task of learning to read. Thus reading is always meaningful and motivation should be greater.

The difficulty of this approach would seem to lie in ensuring that the child is growing in attainment and independence in reading. Further, if a child has already mastered the meaning of the sentence, are we going to be able to gain his full attention to master the spelling pattern of the word and help him to generalize from this instance to other words which have spelling features in common with it?

Bloomfield (1961)[15], Fries (1963)[16] and others have taken an almost diametrically opposed position. They suggest that as the activities of comprehension, evaluation and appreciation are common to all linguistic activities they are not as such part of the reading process. This does not mean that the early stages of reading should not take place using meaningful or enjoyable literature but rather that the emphasis should be upon the mastery of the spelling rules of the language and the attainment of automatic visual recognition of words.

Fries terms this activity the Transfer Stage of reading and he involves the child in matching and discrimination activities of a rather mechanical nature starting with individual letters, then letter pairs and growing through words to sentences. Writing is not a part of the work at this stage and only whole words are spoken orally. The exercises are of the matching type, the child being presented with pairs of letters and saying whether they are the same or different:

I	T
T	T
I	I
T	I
F	T
F	F
E	F

When this has been achieved recognition of letters in groups follows:

IF	IF	
TF	TF	
TF	FT	etc.
FIT	TIF	
FIF	FIE	
FEI	FEI	etc.

Part two of this Transfer Stage is to learn to respond in the same speedy and automatic manner to the spelling patterns of English. Individual letters are never sounded but the whole word is spoken. Words are learned in sequence of their spelling complexity and the contrasts between spelling patterns are pointed out, e.g.

AT – CAT

CAT – RAT

FAT – HAT

The teacher will say each new word as it is introduced and make certain that the child has the word within his language experience.

Spelling rules are built up in a linguistically logical manner from the simple and regular to the complex and infrequently used word. Each new rule being related to previous learning, e.g.

fat – fate – feat – feet

It is easy to see that in its pure form such an approach would yield stilted text, be over mechanical, possibly lacking in motivation and give the child the idea that reading was simply a matter of juggling with signs. It is usual to try to offset the stilted text by an appeal to humour.

It is this latter approach which has greatly influenced the production of materials in America in the past decade.

On the first inspection of such materials, anyone could be excused for making the observation that linguistics has provided nothing new, but is merely a new term for traditional approaches to phonics. There are, however, two major differences.

First, the order in which the sounds are to be learned has grown up rather haphazardly in the phonic approach, and is usually the product of opinion and experience. In a linguistic approach, the order of introduction of spelling patterns is the result of careful analysis of their complexity and regularity.

Second, and rather more important, the traditional phonic approach commenced with the 'sounding out' of the individual letters which made up a word. In a linguistic approach, the child learns to respond from the beginning to groups of letters – individual letters never being given a sound value. Consequently there should be rather less need for unlearning in a linguistic approach than in a phonic one.

Going back to our earlier example; if this had been approached by a phonic method the child would have sounded out the letters *f-a-t,* giving a sound value to each one. When he comes to *fate* he now has to be told that when *a* is followed by the 'magic *e*' the *a* says its name. This would not be necessary in a linguistic approach for here the unit would be *at* and then *ate* and no one letter treated as having a constant sound value.

Modern linguistic studies had, however, been anticipated by some who viewed existing approaches—whether by whole word or phonics—as being inadequate. The best published example of this is to be found in the Phonic-Word method of Daniels and Diack, since incorporated in the *Royal Road Readers* (Hart-Davis Educational). Here a grading of the sounds for difficulty is included but the child is asked only to see the function of each letter in its contribution to the total sound of the word—thus the child does not 'sound out' individual letters. Further, in order to get more readable text, 'sight' words are included. Chall (1967), in an extensive survey of research into methods and materials for reading, suggests that the most promising approach was one which balanced a modified linguistic method with a language experience method. In effect the Phonic-Word method is a modified linguistic approach.

A similar approach to that of Daniels and Diack has been presented by C. Buchanan in *Programmed Reading* (McGraw Hill).

She calls her method the Visuo-Phonic method and it consists of an extensive series of programmed workbooks and story books ending in what is claimed to be the first programmed novel. Linear programming is used even at the pre-reading stage. This means that a very restricted vocabulary is used, and the child cannot practise in his reading the words he may well be learning elsewhere. The most highly structured of the programmed or semi-programmed approaches is to be found in the *Merrill Linguistic Readers* by C. Fries et al. (Charles E. Merrill). These present the child with great security and confidence in the early stages, but it is debatable whether this early regularity helps the child towards independence when he must later face the very inconsistent nature of English spelling.

A sophisticated and comprehensive linguistically based reading scheme is published by Ginn. Called *Reading 360* it is a strong, systematic word-study programme which is linguistic in that it is based on the phonemic and structural features of spoken English. At the early levels, each major phoneme-grapheme correspondence is introduced, and the child is guided from the known (sounds already in his listening and speaking vocabulary) to the unknown (the names and shapes of letters and words). As the child is introduced to the regularities of our language, he is also made aware of language variety and the reasons for it.

Breakthrough to Literacy (Longman) is another linguistically based approach which uses the advantages of language experience approaches. It is, therefore, rather more closely related to the principles of Lefevre than those of Bloomfield and Fries.

Using the Sentence Folder the child builds up from words on card the language he wishes to communicate. In the folder are a number of words already supplied, and then the child can add others. The given words have been selected on the basis of two criteria. Firstly, they are very frequently used in the speech of young children and, secondly they represent the major spelling patterns of the English language. Thus the teacher, whilst working mainly through the child's own language and interest, can structure a developing understanding of spelling patterns. A Word Folder is provided consisting of letters on card with which the child can practise the building of words in a visual manner.

Some teachers using *Breakthrough to Literacy* are using it simply as a means of helping the child to represent his spoken language in print. The lack of attention to work which can be drawn from the scheme, to enable the child to learn the spelling patterns of English, reduces greatly the possibilities of the material. It is very much a 'starter' set of materials in comparison with the more structured approaches described above, and its success depends rather more on the effectiveness of the teacher's usage of it than on the materials themselves. This points to a very obvious difference between British and American materials. The latter are wide ranging, detailed, carefully structured and very extensive. British materials are brief in comparison and allow the teacher much more room to suit materials to her own personality and beliefs. This freedom, however, means that rather more understanding and work is necessary on the part of the teacher using British published materials.

C. Linguistic Contexts for the Use of Phonics in the Teaching of Reading — A Suggested Method
Theodore H. MacDonald

Fallacies in Flesch's Attack

In the 1950s the book *Why Johnny Can't Read* by Rudolf Flesch aroused bitter controversy in America about the teaching of reading by its sweeping claims that useless and untested methods had somehow been foisted on the public by a cunningly contrived cartel of educationists and publishers.

As such, the book served a valuable purpose; for anything which can provoke such wide interest in the basic education of our children, an interest usually conspicuous by its absence, is to be highly commended. Moreover, any teacher reading Flesch's thesis, that virtually all reading problems would vanish if only reading were taught by phonics, would recognize that the argument (although incredibly simplistic) is worthy of scrutiny.

Flesch was on shaky ground indeed when he argued that older-style methods of teaching reading (he commends the old Beacon Readers, for instance) were far and away more effective than the 'look-say' systems popular in the 1940s and early 1950s. Statistics on the score are so incomplete as to render any such comparison meaningless. More seriously, he then went on to argue that this supposed superiority of older systems was due to the fact that they were phonic. Analysis of these older schemes will hardly fail but to surprise a modern teacher at the amount of direct non-phonic word recognition demanded of the pupil. The phonics, although very obviously present, required a high degree of contextual reading ability obtained through familiarity with many non-phonic word shapes. As well, what phonics teaching did take place was almost entirely based on alphabetical spelling, so that between the visual impact of the letter shape and its phonic sound value was interposed the name of the letter. This rendered phonic analysis much more difficult than it need have been.

Potential Teaching Value of Phonics

Despite all this, however, Flesch's book was successful in getting the message across that the English language was not so irascible as proponents of pure 'look-say' approaches had seemed to believe. Only about 13% of English words defy phonic analysis in some respect and of this only about 25% (or 3% of the total) are so at variance with standard phonics as not to be recognizable in context. For instance, consider the word 'was'.

Attacked on the basis of standard phonics, it would emerge as 'was' rhyming with 'as' — obviously an incorrect pronunciation. However, in context, its meaning is usually ascertainable: 'Ben was at home'. The same can be said for such slight irregulars as 'father', 'mother', 'almost', and even 'care', 'dare', etc. However, a systematic instruction in phonics, including long and short vowels, the rule of terminal 'e' and such phonemes as 'ing', 'ink', 'th', 'ch', etc, would almost surely be useless against such members of the '3% irascible' as: 'laugh', 'though', etc.

If one could rely only on the percentages of 'phonic', 'nearly phonic' and 'non-phonic' words in our language, then a considerable argument could still be mounted for reading instruction being virtually totally phonics-oriented, with small lists of non-phonic sight words being sprinkled in from time to time.

Indeed, one of the backlashes of Flesch's book appearing in print was a number of attempts to organize the teaching of reading along these lines. What could seem more logical?

What indeed, except that two factors had been ignored in this rather simplistic analysis:

1. The 13% of almost-phonic or non-phonic words mentioned by Flesch include almost half the words listed by A.I. Gates *(A Reading Vocabulary for Primary Grades, Bureau of Publications, Columbia University)* as most frequently used by children from the ages of five to nine years. In other words, for all intents and purposes, if we are to embark on the teaching of reading by phonics in primary school, we must reckon on only about 50% of words used being 'unlocked' by phonic techniques.
2. The words that are easily 'unlocked' by simple phonics can be used to make sentences in the strict definition of the word, but most of such sentences do not correspond to commonly known or used linguistic patterns, e.g. 'The fat dog had a slug in a net.'

Attempts to Develop Reading Linguistically

It was probably the realization of this last difficulty that initially led educators to throw their hands up in despair and to 'throw the baby out with the bathwater' in the development of look-say methods of teaching reading. However, this alternative too had its difficulties. Reading vocabularies had to be kept discouragingly small, if the capacity for children to remember shapes and patterns of whole words was not to be overtaxed. This not only greatly interfered with the ease with which pupils could acquire the habit of reading widely for pleasure (outside the controlled vocabularies of the readers) but it made writing almost a subtle art-form, for without the obvious link between spelling, phonics and speech, there is little incentive to write freely. The risks of making an undecipherable mistake are too great. The sorts of spelling mistakes that a phonically-trained child makes are usually easily deciphered.

Thus, even in look-say schemes, phonics has to be introduced somewhere along the line — if this is not done very early, the pupil has become so used to 'guessing' at whole words that it is difficult to train him to slow down sufficiently to analyse the individual letters of words he does not recognize. Moreover, the initial stages of phonic analysis are painfully slow and tedious — not something likely to enhance a child's enjoyment of reading once he has been introduced to the other approach.

These considerations led, up into the 1950s, to the use of what educationists came to refer to as 'incidental phonics'. By this process children were (it was hoped) led to 'discover' the rules of phonics — such details as the rule of 'e', suffixes and prefixes, etc. However, such a leisurely approach to the most important single technique for decoding written words could not hope to open the world of books and of free reading quickly enough. It must not be forgotten that the vast majority of children's books, excluding those written with controlled vocabularies and specifically for school use, require as wide a range of phonic analysis techniques as do books written for adult readers. Taken to its logical conclusion, then, incidental phonics would not equip a child to read, say, *Grimm's Fairy Tales* until he was about 15 years old!

What all this boils down to is the need for a method of teaching reading which:

a) quickly equips the child to read independently so that he can have access to the literature relevant and interesting to his age group and which he might freely choose if he were able to read;

b) remains linguistically meaningful throughout the largest part of the skill-acquisition stage so that the child's interest is engaged and so that the goals of learning are always fairly immediate.

This would suggest the need to evolve some combination of phonics teaching (for speed in acquiring the mechanics of independent reading) with attention to the linguistic contexts in which easy phonic words can be set so as to sustain interest.

The Bloomfield System

In 1961, the late American linguist Leonard Bloomfield[17] developed a system in which he attempted to meet the two criteria set out above. Without doubt his massive work (465 pages of graduated phonic blend exercises and idiomatic sentences using accumulated phonic rules!) is the most comprehensive approach to the subject available. Although intended for use with young children (it even works effectively with pre-schoolers) this writer has found the presentation didactic in the extreme. Perhaps this is unavoidable, but it embodies very little intrinsic motivation for the young child. However, it is certainly the best single approach to the teaching of remedial reading cases.

The present author has evolved an approach which he has used with pronounced success with remedial reading cases and in the initial teaching of reading to younger children; it is described in the pages that follow.

An Eclectic System

One can consider the development of reading skills to pass through clearly defined stages, each successive stage depending upon a firm mastery of the preceding one.

Stage I — The Letters

The child is taught to associate each lower case letter with one and only one sound (the capitals can be introduced later when he has thoroughly understood the use of sounds to make blends). Wherever possible this one and only sound should not involve a tailing vowel sound. Thus 'f' should be made with the lower lip tucked under the front teeth with air expelled through the slit. With b, c, d, g, h, k, p, q, t, w, x, y, a bit of a tailsound is unavoidable. The vowels should be linked at this stage with their *short* sounds only. No further work should be done until, using a flashcard for each letter, the child can call out the appropriate sound *and* pick out the appropriate flash-card in response to the teacher presenting a sound.

Stage II — Non-Word Consonant-Vowel-Consonant Blends

ba—, be— (pronounced as in 'bed'), bi—, bo—, bu—, ca—, co—, cu— ('ce' and 'ci' omitted because of the confusion with soft 'c'), da—, de—, di—, do— (as in 'dog'), du—, etc.

Using one flashcard for each, drill for fluency in recognition. It will take some time, for instance, before the child can respond directly to each of these, without laboriously sounding out each letter and then combining them. Once fluency has been attained in this way, work on the blends consisting of vowel first followed by consonant.

Meaning can be attached to this crucial stage by having the child look at pages of print in his story books and pick out the blends he recognizes in words. Likewise, a contrived version of 'I spy', can be played in which the pupil says 'I spy with my little eye something beginning with this flashcard', whereupon he holds up, say, the flashcard 'la' for a lamp. Now teach the child to recognize and write the capital letters.

Stage III — Contrived Sentences Using Short Phonic Words

This stage should be dwelled on only long enough to use combinations of all the Stage II blends, but not so long that the child's sense of natural sentence utterance is strained: e.g.

Pat   can   fan   Dan.

In so far as this is possible, meaning should be ascribed to these sentences by having the child draw pictures above or beside them. Naturally, considerable time should be spent in drill on the isolated words before they are put in a sentence. NOTE: No 'sight' words have yet been introduced, such as 'the'. These will come later.

Stage IV — Consonant--Consonant Blends

These are: bl, br, cl, cr, dr, fl, fr, gl, gr, pl, pr, sl, sm, st, tr. They are best exemplified by their use in words — bless, brat, etc. The sounds 'ch', 'sh' and 'th' have to be taught as separate entities and flashcards should be made for them.

Reading at this point should involve the child working out words in the context of stories being read aloud, the teacher carefully selecting words that can yield to the limited powers of phonic analysis available to the child. The writing of dictated words using these blends is also a valuable exercise. A greater variety of sentences can now be made up by the resourceful teacher for the child to read: e.g.

'Dot and Nat did not thank Mum.'

Stage V — More Blends to Memorize

The collection of flashcards bearing blends that must be known *at sight* will greatly increase during this stage, but so also will the scope for reading words and sentences. The sounds are:

ee, ea, oo, oor (as in 'poor', 'door'), ai,
air, ay, oa, oar, ou, ow, aw, au, oy, oi.

When these sounds have been mastered in isolation and in simple words, two-syllable words can be introduced. This author has found that the best way to explain the idea of syllables is in terms of beats with a clenched fist on a table. The child should practise 'beating the syllables' of polysyllabic words spoken clearly to him by the teacher. In applying this to reading, try to cultivate the habit of sounding out and enunciating *one syllable at a time* and *then* putting the whole word together. The word 'the' should be introduced at this stage to accord greater flexibility to the types of sentences that can be constructed for the pupil to read. The *names* of the letters of the alphabet can now be learned.

Stage VI — The Most Common Irregular Words

Such suffixes as: −es, −d, −ed, −ing, −ink, −nk, −ng, −le, −y. Words such as: to, of, was, be, do, one, says, said, are, were, I, you, he, she, we, they. Such contractions as: −n't.

It cannot be emphasized enough that the learning of reading can become a singularly barren exercise for the pupil unless, along with the bare mechanics of the phonic system and its drills, considerable attention is paid to linguistically uncontrived reading material. Since much of this is as yet inaccessible to the pupil, reliance must be placed on reading aloud to him. However, out of passages that have already been read aloud, and which clearly evinced interest, the teacher can increasingly isolate words, phrases and whole sentences which the child can be asked to decipher from the printed page. This serves a valuable purpose for, not only does it drill facility in phonics, but it encourages the child to read with natural intonation and fluency.

Stage VII — Long Vowel Sounds

The conditions under which the vowel sounds like its letter name. The rule of 'e' and exceptions.

Stage VIII — Irregular Vowel Sounds and Irregular Words Generally

Care, bear, danger, steak, −ar, −or, −ur, −er, −ir, −alt, wash, snow, by, sky, my, new, head, etc. By the time this level is reached the child will now be reading simple books on his own. He will continue to encounter words he has never seen before and which he cannot work out, in which case he must learn them by sight. But even among these words, some order can be imposed by considering *classes* of such irregular words — e.g. words with 'ough' in them, etc.

The four rules of thumb for the sound of 'y':

a) y at the beginning of a word — yes.
b) y in the middle of a word — system.
c) y at the end of a one-syllable word — sty.
d) y at the end of a multi-syllable word — puppy.

Conclusion

In gradually developing this eclectic approach to the teaching of reading, the author has been conscious of the sterility of teaching which results if a single teaching method is relied upon unswervingly and over a great span of time. Thus, this system is intended to inculcate thoroughly the obvious advantages of phonics while at the same time providing scope for digression into writing, imitative reading, etc. This system has been used successfully in a variety of primary schools and in the teaching of remedial reading.

4 The Dependent Reader

Teaching reading as a subject rather than a means for communication can be deadly for children. No one reads *reading*. He reads *something* — letters, books, poems, stories, newspapers — and he reads with a purpose. Each reading experience with children should have meaningful content, a purpose obvious to the child, and pleasant associations. [1]

The dependent reader is a child who has not yet acquired the basic skills of word recognition to a degree where he has power over words. He is dependent on the teacher for both *materials* and *methods* to develop these skills. It is important to realize that such children are not restricted to infant classes but occur throughout the whole school.

An effective programme for the dependent reader must maintain and expand the child's interest while developing word recognition and comprehension skills by systematic, planned instruction.

Skill development during this stage must involve both a vertical development and a horizontal reinforcement of all skill areas. In teaching skills it is necessary to recognize three stages of development:
- ☐ Introduction.
- ☐ Period of practice or reinforcement.
- ☐ Mastery or confidence.

Even children at apparently the same reading level will be at different stages of development within different skill areas. Consequently, fluid grouping for purposes of instruction is essential. Group instruction is valuable provided that the teacher is sensitive to the needs of individual children within the group.

Skills to be Developed:

A. Word Identification
B. Comprehension
C. Oral and Silent Reading
D. Appreciation

A. Word Identification

The following diagram illustrates the various skills incorporated in 'word identification'. While there is no one method which is best for the systematic development of word identification skills, there is need for carefully planned, definite instruction in all the skill areas.

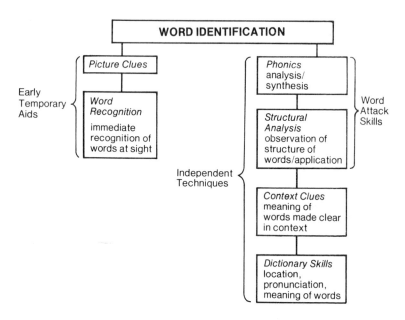

1. Picture Clues

In the first readers of basic reading schemes the illustrations should be planned to give clues to the text. If they do not, children cannot be criticized for saying what *ought* to be in the text rather than what is printed.

In some phonic reading schemes illustrations are omitted because the authors feel that pictures distract rather than help the learner.

Ensure that picture clues on indicator cards, charts and all reading material are appropriate and helpful.

2. Word Recognition

A sight vocabulary can be built incidentally during work in all areas of the curriculum, using charts, labels and notices. It is begun during the pre-reading programme with the introduction of 'Interest in Print' activities.

The development of a sight vocabulary enables a child to gain early the satisfaction of reading simple, but interesting material. This is highly motivating if the context is meaningful in terms of his needs and interests. It can be discouraging and boring if the vocabulary of the readers is so rigidly controlled and repetitious that there is no story line.

The order of introduction of vocabulary in the basic reading scheme is usually listed in the back of the reader and in the Teacher's Manual.

Teaching Sight Words

It is important to include activities for *both* recognition and meaning. Select from this list:

☐ Introduce and use the word in context orally.
☐ Write the word and illustrate it if possible (indicator card).
☐ Write the word in a sentence. Children can suggest sentences (different meanings and shades of meaning).
☐ Isolate the word, write it on a flashcard.
☐ Include the word in matching exercises — picture/word.
☐ Include the word in flashcard games.
☐ Multi-sensory activities should be included:
   — tracing in the air, on the arm, on the floor
   — write, trace and illustrate the word
   — miming activities.
☐ Locate the word in a picture dictionary.

Basic Sight Vocabulary and Key Words

A sentence or word method does not allow for sufficient repetition of the same words and ignores the importance of words in common use. Attempts have been made to overcome these failings by the parallel teaching of both a basic reading scheme and a basic list of sight vocabulary words:

☐ *The Dolch Basic Sight Vocabulary* (220 words). These words can be taught using flashcards or charts. However, a

major criticism is that they are often taught as separate
entities with little consideration being given to either
meaning and use in context or *relevance to the selected
reading scheme.*

☐ *McNally & Murray Key Words and the Teaching of
Reading* (300 words). The idea that children learn to read
more easily and quickly if the first words that they learn to
recognize are the most used words in the language is the
basis for *The Ladybird Key Words Readers.* (McNally and
Murray, *Key Words to Literacy and the Teaching of
Reading).*

Resources

Basic Words Lotto; Keywords Lotto; Picture Word Lotto (Galt).
Word Picture Links (Galt).
300 Common Words (Kiddicraft Games).
Betty Root Reading Games (Hart Davis).
Ladybird Key Words Readers and *Ladybird Key Words List* (Ladybird
    Books).
Oxford Colour Readers (Reading age 6-8, Interest age 8-14) (OUP).
Adventures in Reading; Adventures in Writing (Series); *Crossword Puzzles*
    (Reading age 5-9, Interest age 8-14) (OUP).
Oxford Junior Workbooks (OUP).
Make a Good Start (Mills and Boon).
Colour Snap (Good Reading).
Elephant Game (Good Reading).
Opposites (Macdonald).
The materials listed below are all published by Philip and Tacey.
My First Word Book
Positional Words and Picture Matching Cards
Basic Words Snap Game
Basic Word Lotto; Action and Picture Word Matching Cards
Three of a Kind Strip Books

3. Word Attack Skills

The use of phonics is a complex matter. There is much more
involved in phonic competence than simply recognizing the sounds of
letters or letter groups. There are at least four separate skills involved
in the total phonic process: visual discrimination, auditory
discrimination, blending and contextual application.[2]

Many children fail in reading because they have no knowledge
of phonics whatever. Although a child may have acquired
quite a large sight vocabulary, and may, in addition, be able

to 'guess' some new words he meets by use of contextual clues, he will often be confronted with words which he cannot recognize by these means. A knowledge of phonics would enable a child to read many, though not all, such words. Children need regular and systematic training in phonics at appropriate stages in the process of learning to read.

A Suggested Progression of Phonic Development
- ☐ Pre-phonics (readiness stage).
- ☐ Phoneme (sound) — symbol association.
- ☐ Blending two and three graphemes (letters, letter-combinations) to make words — simple, regular words: cat, dog.
- ☐ Consonant clusters (e.g. initial 'fr' — frog; final 'mp' — jump).
- ☐ Vowel and consonant digraphs (e.g. 'sh' — shop).,
- ☐ Extended knowledge of above: more difficult combinations (e.g. 'a-e' — brave; 'air' — chair; 'ge' — cage; 'tch' — match),
- ☐ Indefinite vowel sounds (e.g. 'o' — today; 'ai' — mountain).

N.B. Extend by means of structural analysis throughout the progression (e.g. skip, skips, skipped, skipping).

Resources

New Chelsea Pictorial Alphabet (Philograph).
Phonic Word Study Cards (Galt).
N. Worthy and M. Rees, *Over the Stile* (Wheaton).
Word Games (SRA).
Schoolhouse (SRA).
Pictures for Sounds (ESA).
M. Hooton, *The First Reading and Writing Scheme* (Heinemann Educational): Teachers' Manual, Practice Book, Dictionary, 4 Wall charts.
Word Families Series (Philograph).
A.E. Tansley: *Sounds Sense Series* (E.J. Arnold).
Language in Action Resource Books: Alphabet Level and Levels 1, 2, 3, (Macmillan Education).
Royal Road Reading Scheme, and *Teacher's Manual* (Hart Davis).
Tempo Readers (Longman) — carefully controlled vocabulary, phonic based, for older dependent readers.
Bangers and Mash (Longman) — fourteen graded phonic readers, notes for the teacher.
Jabberwocky (Longman) — card game.
Programmed Reading Kit (Holmes McDougall) — Games: First Letter Bingo, Post Boxes, Pattern Bingo, Fable Cards, Snakes Games.

The materials listed below are all published by Philip and Tacey.
New Colet Pictures and Sounds Matching Cards
Royal Road Reading Apparatus
Consonant — Vowel Blend Matching Cards
Phonogram Workbooks

4. Structural Analysis

Children learn to recognize words by their basic structure. This work should be linked with the phonics programme. Collections of words can be made on charts or in booklets:

- ☐ Word endings: s, ed, ing, er;
  jump, jumps, jumped, jumping, jumper.
- ☐ Plurals: boy, boys; box, boxes; ox, oxen; fairy, fairies; knife, knives; fish, fish; mouse, mice; man, men; fungus, fungi.
- ☐ Compound words: sunset, everyone, goldfish, newspaper.
- ☐ Possessives: girl, girl's; girls'.
- ☐ Contractions: she's, we're, I'll, wouldn't.
- ☐ Syllabication: dis-cov-er, rel-a-tive.

5. Context Clues

Intelligent guessing and use of context clues are a part of a mature approach to reading. Even in the dependent stage of reading the child can be encouraged to use context clues. He can be taught that when he comes to an unknown word he should read on to the end of the sentence to see if he can guess it. In the early stages of reading, use the vocabulary of the basic readers in different contexts as blackboard or assignment card exercises to develop the recognition of words in different contexts.

6. Combining Word Identification Techniques

Flexibility in word attack is important. A good reader is not dependent on any one way of attacking words. He has mastered several techniques and uses those that best fit the situation. Teachers can do a child a disservice by telling the child immediately when he stops at an unfamiliar word. Teach him that when a word is unknown he should attack it himself, first by the meaning of the sentence, and then by phonics and structural analysis.

7. Dictionary Use

The child at the dependent level of reading begins to learn how to use a dictionary to help in reading and writing activities. Firstly, when he needs to spell words in his creative writing, he learns to locate them on charts around the room, and then he graduates to using simple dictionaries as well. Children need guidance in use of dictionaries — demonstration and discussion in meaningful situations. It is important that dictionary usage is not associated with boredom, drudgery, anxiety and meaningless exercises. The children's motive for using a dictionary should be curiosity about words, and their quest should be rewarded with satisfaction.

- ☐ Wall charts
  - vocabulary lists in interest groupings: classroom pet; Social Studies topic,
  - words in phonic or structural groupings.
- ☐ Alphabetic files — words on cards in boxes.
- ☐ Class dictionary — 'Our Book of Interesting Words' — add words from stories, poems, broadcasts, science, excursions.
- ☐ Personal dictionary — compiled with the teacher's help: words that the child needs in his written expression.
- ☐ Commercially prepared dictionaries:
  Picture Dictionaries
  - Pictures and Sounds abc (Philograph).
  - A First/Second Ladybird Picture Dictionary (Ladybird Books).
  - Chambers Young Set Dictionary One.
  More Advanced Dictionaries
  - Chambers Young Set Dictionary Two, Three.
  - English Picture Dictionary (OUP).
  - Longman's First English Dictionary.

Tests: Word Identification

Schonell Test R1: graded word reading (Oliver and Boyd).
Burt Word Reading Test (Hodder and Stoughton).

See also: *Reading Tests and Assessment Techniques* P.D. Pumfrey (Hodder and Stoughton).

Further Reading

J. Downing, A. L. Brown and J. Sceets, *Words Children Want to Use*, Handbook to Chambers Dictionaries (Chambers).

D.H. Stott, *Roads to Literacy* (Holmes McDougall).

J.C. Daniels and H. Diack, *Progress in Reading in the Infant School* (Nottingham Institution of Education, University of Nottingham).

J. Hughes, *Phonics and the Teaching of Reading* (Evans).

D. Moyle, *The Teaching of Reading* (Ward Lock Educational, 4th edn).

B. Comprehension

Various comprehension skills are initiated in the junior primary years. Reading for comprehension, rather than simply recognizing words, should be encouraged from the beginning. A wealth of experience and a mastery of oral language are prerequisites for reading comprehension.

The following skills can be taught:

☐ Reading to grasp the main idea, e.g. suggest a title for a passage.

☐ Reading to select important details, e.g. sentence completion, draw a plan or a map.

☐ Reading to follow directions, e.g. recipe, directions for making a puppet.

☐ Reading for sequential order, e.g. read and re-tell, dramatize, make a filmstrip, rearrange sentences.

☐ Organization of what is read; a great deal can be learnt from the teacher's example and demonstration in the dependent reading stage. The teacher shows how to locate material through the index and table of contents, how to scan and find specific information, and gives assistance in making brief reports on social studies or science topics.

Tests: Comprehension

GAP Reading Comprehension Test (Heinemann Educational).

Schonell Test R2 and R3 (Oliver and Boyd).

Edinburgh Reading Tests (Hodder and Stoughton).

See also P. D. Pumfrey, *Reading: Tests and Assessment Techniques* (Hodder and Stoughton).

Simple Informational Books

Non-fiction series with limited vocabulary and attractive illustrations are useful in the development of comprehension skills, especially when provision is made for appropriate culminating activities: cooking, science/nature experiments, art/craft activities, lists, charts, posters, reports, drama, experience books.

Macdonald Starters and *Starters Activities* (Macdonald Educational). *Living and Growing* (Macmillan). *See How it Grows* (Macmillan). *First Interest Books* (Ginn). *Time for Cooking* (Ginn).

Further Reading

Kathleen Hester, *Teaching Every Child to Read* (Harper and Row).
Albert Harris, *How to Increase Reading Ability* (Longman, 5th edn).

Resources

The handbook accompanying the reading scheme in use should be consulted at every stage so that the best use is made of the materials (workbooks, stencil masters, assignment cards, etc.).
English in the Making (Longman).
Reading Skill Cards (McGraw Hill).
Ladybird English Work Cards (Ladybird Books).

C. Oral and Silent Reading

Sometimes schools are so tightly scheduled that there is no time for a child to just sit down and read. [3]

All reading is oral in the beginning. Gradually children read sub-vocally, and finally they are able to read silently. The time needed to master this skill varies, and, while children can be encouraged to read 'quietly', they should not be put under pressure to read silently when they are not ready to do so.

1. Oral Reading

Even when silent reading has been achieved, opportunities should be given for oral reading, for purposes of evaluation and assistance, and for the development of oral reading skills. (However, bear in mind that most adult reading will be silent, so do not place undue importance on oral reading.)

Reading to the teacher

In the early stages, reading to the teacher (or to any adult) is very important to the child; he will probably want to read every page of every reader to her. Later on this is not necessary. Insistence on hearing and marking every page can frustrate competent readers, especially those who read at home.

The child should have time for preparation beforehand.

The teacher should listen attentively and encourage the child to read expressively to convey thought and feeling. Assistance in understanding punctuation may be needed for a long time.

The teacher notes:

☐ Fluency — ability to read in phrases rather than word by word.

☐ Comprehension — ability to follow a train of thought.

☐ Expression — voice indicating direct speech and mood.

☐ Word attack — ability to find out new or difficult words.

Tests can be given informally after the reading:

☐ Word recognition — ask the child to point to a specific word; or point to a word and ask the child to name it.

☐ Comprehension — ask a question about the reading passage.

Note whether re-teaching is necessary (e.g. difficult vocabulary).

For ease and fluency in reading encourage children sometimes to read material more simple than the basic reader.

Reading to parents

From the beginning provision can be made for the child to take readers home to read to his family. Capitalize on early enthusiasm to inculcate a reading habit. The interest and assistance of parents and siblings is invaluable in providing motivation and practice.

Audience reading

While 'reading round the class' is not beneficial, sometimes a child can read to others if he wants to. He can select, prepare and read, preferably from material unfamiliar to the other children.

Taking turns in a small group

In a small group of similar reading ability taking turns to read can be both valuable and pleasurable. Children can ask each other comprehension questions afterwards, or they can prepare to dramatize the story.

2. Silent Reading

Silent reading gives the child satisfaction as he can read at his own pace. He can relax because he does not have to consider expression, enunciation, punctuation, fluency and phrasing. He can 'skip' a word that he does not know, and go back over several sentences for meaning.

Provide many books at each level of reading difficulty and work out an efficient borrowing system so that the children can borrow books regularly and frequently.

Some children do not have either facilities or encouragement to read at home. They need *time* and *encouragement* for private personal reading *at school* if they are to become readers for life.

Resources

Listening and Reading (booklets and recordings), Stages 1 and 2 (Penguin).
Magic Circle Books (Ginn).
Publisher's lists, e.g. *Puffin List* (Penguin); *New Windmill Series* (Heinemann Educational).

Further Reading

See the handbook of the basic reading scheme in use.
A. Chambers, *Introducing Books to Children* (Heinemann Educational).
P. Hollingdale, *Choosing Books for Children* (Paul Elek).
George Pappas, *Reading in the Primary School* (Macmillan).
A. K. Pugh, *Silent Reading: An Introduction to its Study and Teaching* (Heinemann Educational).

Miscue Analysis

Goodman has said: Miscues are not simply errors. They show more about the learner's strengths than about his weaknesses. In reading, they are the best possible indications of how efficiently and effectively the reader is using the reading process.

Whatever a reader does is caused as he engages in this psycholinguistic process. The reader uses the print and his language competence to get to the meaning. The miscues he makes, reflect what he's doing.

When we teach people to read, we aren't teaching them letter/sound relationships or word-names, or sets of skills. We're

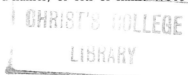

helping them to develop strategies to get to meaning from print which parallel and draw on the ones they use to get from oral language to meaning.

We learn to listen to what miscues a reader makes, what effect they have on meaning, whether the reader corrects when the meaning is lost or disrupted. We find the strengths that the miscues reveal and build on them. We teach for comprehension strategies, confirmation strategies, correction strategies.

We encourage readers at all levels of proficiency to take risks, to use their language competence to guess what would make sense when they're unsure. We rejoice in choice miscues and drop our preoccupation with accuracy and isolatable skills.

The work of Professors Kenneth and Yetta Goodman, international experts on the diagnostic technique of miscue analysis, is significant at many levels.

The Goodman technique of exploring the reading process with individual children has valuable application to both research and classroom practice.

By listening to the oral reading of children and by using a coding system to note *miscues*, an effective analysis of a reader's actual reading can be obtained.

The repetition of types of miscues may then throw light on particular strengths and weaknesses in the readers, as well as on the 'inside operation' of readers generally.

The effectiveness of this analysis depends on the teacher's sensitivity to the child, and upon her knowledge of the reading process itself. The emphasis is on meaning and the child is encouraged to search for the meaning, to become involved in the 'psycholinguistic guessing game' that reading is.

Miscue analysis provides an effective method of recording reading development and diagnosing problems. Miscues are windows on the reading process being used by a particular reader dealing with a particular text. The miscue is observable but through it we see the underlying process that produces it.

In the area of beginning reading the Goodman approach suggests:

☐ A heavier weighting on programmes that have a language experience rationale.
☐ Material that is meaningful to children and linked closely to their interests.
☐ A playing down of strict hierarchical skill-based

programmes that place inflexible emphasis on one aspect of decoding to sound with little relationship to language as it is.

☐ A positive approach to 'remediation', believing that many remedial cases are simply developmental cases in need of nothing more than a sensitive, well-informed teacher and something worthwhile to read.

The Goodman emphasis is upon reading as a part of language activities that human beings use for communication rather than an isolated discipline that can be taught by itself. Effective reading is highly dependent upon what a reader brings to print. Consequently reading for meaning must be the fundamental aim of the activity, whatever the context.

Readers of all ages need to have at their disposal a wide variety of strategies. They make a selection from their repertoire to allow them to reach meaning as quickly and effectively as possible.

Further Reading

K.S. Goodman (ed.), *The Psycholinguistic Nature of the Reading Process* (Wayne State University Press, 1968).

The learner should read a lot. It is important to shower learners with printed material on any subject, to let them explore the unfamiliar and guess at words and meanings. Encourage them to be bold enough to make many mistakes and learn how to correct themselves. At this point in mastering the skill of reading (just beyond the beginning level), a grading system can devastate the learner. It is as if a child who has just learned to take a few steps were punished for falling. To walk well the child must be bold enough to risk falling and not take it too seriously. The same is true for the fledgling readers: they must be encouraged to take chances, make guesses, figure things out for themselves, ask questions and become friendly with the printed word.[4]

D. Appreciation Skills

Children struggling with dreary passages in readers should be systematically regaled and refreshed by passages from literature. Fiction written to be read to young children is every bit as important as that which is written to be read by them.

As the skill (of reading) is being mastered — as it must — an experience of the delights of character, fast flickering action, comedy, word-play, high adventure and myth, to which that skill is the key, is being offered.[5]

Throughout the primary school aural literacy is far ahead of reading literacy — most children can enjoy books that they cannot possibly read themselves. It is most important that, while they are mastering the mechanics of reading, the teacher is reading to them daily, proving that books are pleasurable, adding to their vocabulary, stimulating their imagination, and giving them power over words for use in oral and written expression.

It can take four or five years (or longer) to master the mechanics of reading. A child might be ten before he is a fluent reader, and some children enter secondary school without this mastery. They need all the encouragement and enthusiasm of an understanding teacher so that they do not reject books. Appreciation skills are 'caught' rather than taught at the dependent reader level.

1. Read and Tell Stories

Reading to children is regarded by some people as an 'intelligent indulgence' when it is in fact a 'vital necessity'. (Hildick, *Children and Fiction*, p.80). Money spent on readers and information books is not regarded as wasted, but some teachers and parents do not accord equal value or importance to a large stock of fiction books. Similarly, Hildick says, teachers automatically allocate time for regular reader use, but few give equal time for reading stories *to* children.

Folk tales, myths and legends: e.g. Rhoda Power, *Stories from Everywhere* (Dobson)

Self-contained stories by distinguished authors: e.g. *Author's Choice* (Puffin).

Poetry: e.g. E. Blishen (ed.), *Oxford Book of Poetry for Children*, illustrated by B. Wildsmith (OUP).

2. Sharing Picture-Story Books with Children

Hildick says that good picture books are an excellent introduction to the *feel* of books and to their power to delight. The teacher who reads them is alleviating the insipidity of readers through 'pictorial richness', 'characters more sharply individualized', backgrounds with 'greater authenticity, depth potentiality', and incidents with 'stronger dramatic propensities'. [6]

Picture-story books can be used with senior primary as well as junior primary grades. Some picture-story books have vocabulary and style of writing more suitable for older children; characterization is more complex, and subject matter, themes and ideas are more appropriate for children in middle and senior grades; e.g.

Isaac Singer, *The Fearsome Inn* (Scribner).

Reiner Zimnik, *Drummers of Dreams* (Faber).

T. Ungerer, *The Beast of Monsieur Racine; The Hat; Zeralda's Ogre* (Puffin).

Always leave the picture-story book in an accessible place for individual perusal and enjoyment of detail in illustrations.

3. Adding Depth to Subject Matter

Familiar subjects introduced in readers for infants are neither explored in depth nor developed in any direction. To counteract this superficiality read some stories and poems on the same subjects, but 'exploring them vigorously, viewing them from different, strange, amusing or tragic angles'. (Hildick, op. cit. p.81).

Some basic reading schemes are planned with literature links as an important part of their structure, e.g. the *Scott Foresman Reading Systems* have beautiful books of stories and poetry to read to the children at each level for enrichment.

When folk tales appear in basic readers, introduce children to collections of folk tales, and *tell* folk tales.

4. Select Chapters to Whet the Appetite

Select a book from a series and read one chapter aloud, e.g. read 'Mrs Pepperpot Minds the Baby', a funny episode in Alf Proysen's *Little Old Mrs Pepperpot* (Puffin). There are four books in the Mrs Pepperpot series, so there is scope for children who want to borrow immediately.

5. Serial Reading

Select books that are episodic for serial reading to infants and middle primary years, e.g. Ursula M. Williams, *Gobbolino, the Witch's Cat* (Puffin). Include some stories whose original style and unusual wording are too daunting for most children to read, e.g. Norman Lindsay, *The Magic Pudding* (Puffin).

6. The Library Habit

In some schools, infants are allowed to participate in the school borrowing scheme. Although teaching borrowing skills to young children is tedious and time-consuming, and some books may be lost or damaged, 'the values and outcomes outweigh the disadvantages. The child is able to take home, not only his reader to read to his parents, but also a good picture-story book, e.g. Brian Wildsmith's *The Lion and the Rat* (OUP), for his parents to read to him. Hopefully, he will try to read it for himself, or at least verbalize it and enjoy the pictures.

Apart from its obvious values for children, the infant library borrowing scheme is an excellent way of introducing parents to the beauty and joy of good books for children, and a way of remedying the fact that some parents and relations buy 'rubbish' as gift books for children. The children who benefit most are those not served by a municipal library, and those whose parents do not use a library. This is in line with the latest library trends — taking books to children, rather than children to books.

Gifted Readers — Enrichment

At the time when most of the class are at the dependent reading stage, there will probably be five or six children who are mature readers. Their need for more challenging personal reading can easily be overlooked. Reading interests and tastes can be fostered by encouraging them to read books by outstanding authors. There are many relatively simple novels which have well constructed plots and excellent characterization, written in lively style: e.g.

Gazelle Series (Hamish Hamilton).

Young Puffins (Penguin).

Acorn Library (Bodley Head).

Read Aloud Series (Methuen).

For further ideas see Appreciation Skills p.81.

Further Reading

Wallace Hildick, *Children and Fiction* (Evans).

Joan Cass, *Literature and the Young Child* (Longman).

Nancy Larrick, *A Teacher's Guide to Children's Books* (Charles E. Merrill).

Margaret Meek, et al., *The Cool Web* (The Bodley Head).

5 The Independent Reader

A major task of the primary school is to equip children with sound foundations in the skills of communication — listening, speaking, reading and writing.

The effective reader has at his command a fund of reading skills and abilities — those that he uses to identify unfamiliar words and determine their meaning in context; others that enable him to adjust his reading behaviour in the light of his reading purposes; still others that he uses for critical reading of fiction, non-fiction, explanations and instructions, poetry and drama.

The effective reader brings to his reading broad understandings about the structure and development of his language along with educated attitudes, habits and tastes.

Children's progress in the ability to establish purposes for reading depends to a great extent on the content they are called upon to read. Through a balanced choice of stories, articles, poems and essays, teachers can help children discover that some selections should be read to identify story problems, others to find specific information, still others for sheer enjoyment and so on. Once children have clear purposes for reading, they can readily learn to adjust their reading behaviour to these purposes. With guidance, children will soon discover that an article they are reading for details and an adventure story they are reading for fun cannot be read at the same speed. They soon discover that a poem they are studying to appraise the poet's style and an article they are reading to search out the author's purpose, motive or point of view require different reading techniques.

Teachers should make the most of every opportunity to build both good attitudes and habits. These can largely be developed along with the skills and abilities that go into the act of reading. Certainly all pupils need to strengthen the habits of reading words, sentences and paragraphs carefully, of demanding meaning of what is read, of setting purposes for reading. Beyond such habits of reading is the complex of attitudes and habits that go into critical reading. Because children bring to reading a backlog of experiences they are ready to utilize the skills, abilities and attitudes at their command to meet demands of critical reading. The first requisite for critical reading is an inquiring attitude that leads to continuous evaluation both while reading and after a selection is completed. Sensitivity to the author's purpose is another important aspect, as is the ability to judge the relevancy and authenticity of reading materials. Lastly, an appreciation of fine writing in prose and poetry can be fostered.

Children who love to read are usually excellent readers. Teachers can help children to develop reading tastes and build appreciation of literature.

Advantage can be taken of children's ever broadening interests to encourage independent personal reading. The more children read on their own to satisfy their interests, the more successful they will become, both as readers and as people.

The following skills should be considered:

A. Word Identification.
B. Comprehension.
C. Selective Reading, Study and Locational Skills.
D. Appreciation Skills.

A. Word Identification

The skills initiated in the dependent reader stage should be extended:

1. Visual Clues

Readers.
Language experience projects.
Diagrams, plans and maps.
Language of mathematics and science.
Television.
Commerce: supermarkets, department stores, advertising.

2. Context Clues

'Everything that surrounds the word can be part of the context of the word.' Understanding the various meanings a word may have, and appreciating the fine shades of meaning context may give a word, are skills that develop.

Understanding: synonyms, antonyms, homonyms, figurative language, similes, metaphors.

Language grows and changes: influence of pop culture and advertising.

3. Structural Analysis

By means of structural analysis a reader identifies meaning units in words and sees relationships between inflected or derived forms and their roots. Through these changes our language has acquired much of its great flexibility, enabling a single, central meaning to be modified in several ways.

Continue work begun at the dependent level, and extend: root word plus prefixes and suffixes, inflectional endings and syllabication.

4. Word Attack Skills

Continue the programme begun at the dependent level. While a spelling programme is most valuable to the child for mastery of written expression it also helps him to decode words in his reading.

By the time the children reach the stage of independence there will be widely differing achievement levels in spelling, so individualized materials should be used. Teachers can construct their own materials, or use commercially prepared programmed kits.

5. Dictionary Skills

Skills to be developed include:
☐ Location of words quickly
   — alphabet training
   — inflected forms, e.g. busy, busied
☐ Pronunciation of words
   — diacritical marks, e.g. buy (bī)
   — syllabication, e.g. re'cord

☐ Meaning
 — word in context (select meaning)
 — meaning clear (context of sentence)
☐ Unabridged dictionary information, e.g.
 — bibliographical data
 — geographical locations
☐ Enriched vocabulary
 — derivatives
 — words borrowed from other languages: Latin, Greek, French, Spanish.

Resources

Programmed Spelling Kits:
Spelling Word Power Laboratories (SRA).
Blackwell's Spelling Workshop (Basil Blackwell).

Workbooks, Dictionaries and Lists;
Thorndike-Barnhart Dictionary (Scott Foresman).
Black's Writing Dictionary (A. & C. Black).
Young Set Dictionaries, Three and Four (Chambers).
Marion Saunders, *Take a Word* (Macmillan).
D. & H. Ballance, *What's in a Word?* (E.J. Arnold).
R.J. Hoare, *Planned English* (Ginn).
Ronald Ridout, *Word Perfect*, Books 5-8 (Ginn).
L. Sealey, *Exploring Language* (Nelson).
Building Reading Power (Charles E. Merrill).
Macmillan Spectrum of Skills (Macmillan).
S. A. Stagg, *Spellaway* (Schofield and Sims).
W.D. Wright, *Learn to Spell* (Nelson).
K. Agar, *Collect Your Own Words; Choose Your Own Words* (Cassell).

Further Reading

George Pappas, *Reading in the Primary School* (Macmillan).
A.E. Tansley, *Reading and Remedial Reading* (Routledge and Kegan Paul).
M. Peters, *Diagnostic and Remedial Spelling Manual* (Macmillan).
C. Walker, *Reading Development and Extension* (Ward Lock).

B. Comprehension

The following skills are essential to reading comprehension:

☐ Grasping the general idea or meaning of a passage.
☐ Finding the main idea of
 a) a sentence;
 b) a paragraph;
 c) a page or selection.

☐ Finding the sequence of events or ideas.
☐ Selecting significant details (details supporting the main idea).
☐ Classifying or grouping ideas.
☐ Interpreting facts accurately.
☐ Reaching a conclusion or generalization.
☐ Following directions.
☐ Evaluating ideas for relevancy and authenticity.
☐ Recognizing the mood, tone, or intent of the author.
☐ Recognizing various types of material and understanding the purpose for which the material is read.

There are three levels on which a reader can understand an author's ideas. Each requires skill and practice.

1. Literal Level — 'Reading the lines'

A rearrangement of the sentence structure will give the answer, e.g. The plane landed at Glasgow airport. Where did the plane land?

2. Interpretation Level — 'Reading between the lines'

The reader has to probe for greater depth of meaning. Many facets of meaning can be deduced through interpretation.

☐ Supplying or anticipating answers not stated in the text.
☐ Drawing inferences.
☐ Making generalizations.
☐ Reasoning cause and effect.
☐ Anticipating endings.
☐ Making comparisons.
☐ Sensing motives of a character or an author.

3. Assimilation Level — 'Reading beyond the lines'

Critical reading. The reader evaluates and passes personal judgement on the quality, value, accuracy and truthfulness of what is read.

☐ Encourage children to find the part of a statement that must be true before the rest can be true.

☐ Encourage children to evaluate newspaper reports critically for accuracy, prejudice, bias, propaganda;
Motoring writers' reports on new car models;
Comparing two critics' reports on plays;
Propaganda devices used on radio, television and in newspapers;
Advertising for detergents and appliances.

Appreciation. Children can be encouraged to relate ideas to previous experience and to their own feelings.
☐ How would you feel if you were one of the characters?
☐ What would you do if that happened to you?

Resources

Reading Through Interest (Longman).
Reading With Understanding (Longman).
Macmillan Spectrum of Skills (Macmillan).
Reader's Digest Reading Skill Builders.
New Reading (Reader's Digest Educational Department).
Newslab Kit (SRA).
Reading for Understanding (SRA).
Exploring Language (Nelson).
Growing Up with English (Angus and Robertson).
Comprehension and Study Cards (Wheaton).

Further Reading

James A. Smith, *The Creative Teaching of Reading and Literature in the Elementary School* (Allyn and Bacon).
George Pappas, *Reading in the Primary School* (Macmillan).
L.A. Harris and C.B. Smith, *Reading Instruction through Diagnostic Teaching* (Holt, Rinehart and Winston).
M. Meek et al., *The Cool Web* (The Bodley Head).

C. Selective Reading, Study and Locational Skills

In a culture where much reading material is available and where the average citizen must read a great deal to remain literate in national and world affairs, speed in reading becomes an essential skill. But speed in reading is a skill only if the reader comprehends what he reads. Part of the problem in developing speed in reading is helping the child *think* about what he reads.

The *type of thinking* must help determine the speed. Is he, for instance, reading to think *critically, evaluatively, imaginatively, appreciatively, analytically?* The purpose of reading determines the proper speed of reading. Part of the problem, then, is to help the reader recognize material which should be read with speed and that which must be read slowly. [1]

1. Selective Reading Skill

Scanning: a planned hunt-skip process for finding facts, names, dates, sizes, distances, prices and similar information, e.g. in telephone directory.

Skimming: an organized search to find out quickly what a book, a chapter, or an article is about.

Overviewing: helps decide:
   whether material is worth reading;
   whether it is too difficult to read.

Previewing: a closer look at a book, chapter or article.

Skimming for main ideas: paragraph by paragraph search for main ideas.

Skimming for review: used to recall ideas already forgotten.

   In learning these skills children can be encouraged to discuss and then make lists of material which should be read carefully, and those which may be skimmed: e.g.

Carefully: directions — how to use the tape recorder; science experiment; newspaper article (details, sequence of events).

Quickly: newspaper article (for main idea); stories (leisure reading); TV guide (time of specific programme).

   Habits of more rapid reading often aid comprehension by shifting attention from individual words to phrases and sentences. In *The Creative Teaching of Reading and Literature* (pp. 190-92). Smith makes practical suggestions for helping children develop speed in reading.

2. Locational Skills

In this day of abundant newspapers, magazines, encyclopaedias, dictionaries, reference books, and other kinds of printed matter, skill in finding information is becoming more important.

Basic Skills

Words arranged in alphabetical order — dictionary drill
(telephone directory is very useful).
Index, library catalogue.
Finding a specific page quickly.
Knowledge of content of reference books.
Interpreting information.
Making use of the information.

Information about Books

The child should know the parts of a book — preface or
introduction, table of contents, lists of maps or illustrations,
chapter headings, sub-headings, index.

Reference Books

Knowledge of what is contained in reference books and the
organization of material.
Ability to decide in which reference book the information is
likely to be found.
Skill in finding the information.

   Many of the above skills are taught by the school librarian,
but should be reinforced by the class teacher.

   It is difficult to separate study skills and locational skills
because they both involve the content subjects, but if they are
developed by the teacher, the child learns:

   The powers of discrimination and rejection;
   The ability to summarize;
   The logical presentation of notes and materials;
   The ability to increase rate of reading, and recall.

Resources

Research Lab (SRA)
Reader's Digest Reading Skill Builders.
Content subject materials — e.g. Social Studies, Science.
Topical information from newspapers and magazines.
Encyclopaedias.
Globes, atlases, street directories, road maps, weather maps.
Telephone directories.
Graphs and charts of various kinds.
Film and filmstrip catalogues.
Television programme guides.

Further Reading

James A. Smith, *The Creative Teaching of Reading and Literature in the Elementary School* (Allyn and Bacon).

L.A. Harris and C.B. Smith, *Individualizing Reading Instruction* (Holt, Rinehart and Winston).

D. *Appreciation Skills*

When the child reaches the level of independent reading, some parents and teachers think that there is now no longer any need for adult reading and telling of stories. In fact, at this stage the need is as great, if not greater.

Children who enjoy reading will pursue their reading interests, perhaps in one or two main directions. It is important that they meet a great variety of literature, so the teachers can select novels from different categories for serial reading, as well as short stories, myths, legends, epics, ballads, and poetry of different kinds. The child who reads animal stories, or family adventure exclusively, will find a new world opening up to him when the teacher selects from other categories, e.g.

Fantasy and Magic: L.M. Boston, *The Children of Green Knowe* (Faber).

Historical Fiction: Rosemary Sutcliff, *Circlet of Oak Leaves* (Antelope-Hamish Hamilton).

Science Fiction: Madeline L'Engle, *A Wrinkle of Time* (Puffin).

Myths and Legends: Barbara L. Picard, *Stories of King Arthur and his Knights* (OUP).

Poetry: Ruth Manning-Sanders, *A Bundle of Ballads* (OUP).

Stories which present some difficulty, perhaps in language, setting or length, can be very enjoyable as a shared experience of listening and discussion, building group morale, e.g.

Kenneth Grahame, *The Wind in the Willows* (Methuen).

J.R.R. Tolkien, *The Hobbit* (Allen and Unwin).

J. Meade Falkner, *Moonfleet* (Puffin).

M. Balderson, *When Jays Fly to Barbmo* (OUP).

Patricia Wrightson, *The Rocks of Honey* (Puffin).

While she needs to respect and encourage the child's interests, the teacher can introduce him to imaginative writing, excellent characterization and worthwhile themes.

Thus he gradually assimilates standards by which he can evaluate and select for himself. He learns to recognize hackneyed presentation of themes and character stereotypes.

Book Selection

Children are not born with a feel for literature any more than for art and music. Therefore teachers need to be able to select books to ensure that children meet a wealth of worthwhile literature. Book selection is a time-consuming task requiring critical appreciation and a knowledge of children and their interests. While book lists are helpful there is no substitute for wide and continuous reading of children's books. (See Aids to Book Selection p.82).

Children's Literature and Creative Drama

The child's natural interest in the use of voice and movement to convey meanings should be enouraged throughout the literature programme. It is easy to stultify this interest by using drama books and scripted drama. While dramatization of stories or episodes in books has a place, children should be encouraged to create their own mimes and plays. Literature can be a source of inspiration:

Creation of another episode or adventure;

A different ending or turn of events caused by the arrival of another character;

Association with the children's experience — imagine that the situation described in the book happened in your town.

Children's Literature and Creative Response

Books serve as wellsprings of creative effort for many children. A beautiful passage in a story may stimulate one child to write an original poem, a well-illustrated book may challenge another youngster to paint or do sculpturing. Other feelings in books may lead to dancing, the dramatization of stories and/or singing. [2]

Teachers who regularly read stories and poetry find that children respond imaginatively in creative activities. Often they do not require specific direction or topic suggestions.

Children who read humour and nonsense, such as Norman Hunter's *The Incredible Adventures of Professor Branestawm* (Puffin) are able to imagine possibilities for writing and drama. The power of words to evoke atmosphere enables the child to participate through superb writing in a wonderful fantasy such as Lucy Boston's *The Sea Egg* (Faber). This assists his vocabulary development, enriches his oral and written expression, and generates ideas for art and music activities. When a child identifies with characters and situations in books, and makes associations with his own experience, he is able to discuss motives, ideas and actions, e.g. A. Rutgers van der Loeff, *Avalanche* (Puffin).

The following materials use the child's interest in books to provide enriching experiences, encouraging investigation and creative response:

Resources
Ann Evans, *Blackwell's Literature Cards* (Basil Blackwell) — emphasis on oral and written expression activities — senior primary and junior secondary.

W. Martin and G. Vallins, *Exploration Drama* (Evans Bros) — thematic drama material — refers to literature and art.

Storyhouse (OUP).

Scope for Reading (Holmes MacDougall).

Further Reading
C.S. Huck and D.Y. Kuhn, *Children's Literature in the Elementary School* (Holt, Rinehart and Winston).

Robert Whitehead, *Children's Literature: Strategies of Teaching* (Prentice-Hall).

T.W. Haggitt, *Working with Language* (Basil Blackwell).

The creative teaching of literature can build a colourful vocabulary that will assist each child to express himself better. It can help children build a set of standards and values regarding creative writing.[3]

E. Aids to Book Selection
The skilled author does not write differently or less carefully for children just because he thinks they will not be aware of style or language . . . The author of children's literature must know the essentials of fine writing and apply this knowledge to children's books.[4]

1. Criteria for Selection of Books
Plot
☐ Does the book tell a good story?
☐ Is the story believable in terms of either reality or imagination?
☐ Is there action and suspense?
☐ Is it plausible and credible without relying on coincidence and contrivance?

Content and Theme

☐ Is the story appropriate for the age and the stage of development for which it has been written?

☐ Is the story worth telling?

☐ Does it avoid moralizing and yet help to give children a sense of values and purpose?

☐ Do justice and truth prevail?

Characterization

☐ Are the characters real and convincing?

☐ Can one see both their strengths and weaknesses?

☐ Has the author avoided types?

☐ Do the characters develop and grow?

Style

☐ Does the style fit the story and the subject matter?

☐ Is it clear and understandable with dialogue suitable to the characters?

☐ Is there an exciting and imaginative use of words and a richness of expression?

(Selected from Huck and Kuhn, *Children's Literature in the Elementary School*, pp. 9-18).

Further Reading

G. Fox, G. Hammond, T. Jones, F. Smith and K. Sterck (eds), *Writers, Critics and Children* (Heinemann Educational).

2. Book Lists

Recent Children's Fiction, available from Iain Ball, Avon House North, St James Barton, Bristol.

A Guide to Book Lists and Bibliographies for Use in Schools, Peter Platt, School Library Association (SLA), Victoria House, 29-31 George Street, Oxford.

B. Clark, *Children's Stories: fiction, verse and picture books for primary and middle schools* (SLA).

O. Warren and G. Barton, *Fiction, Verse and Legend: a guide to the selection of imaginative literature for the middle and secondary school years* (SLA).

Bibliographies in children's literature books, e g Joan Cass, *Literature and the Young Child* (Longman).

Publishers' Lists. Publishers' lists can be useful if used critically.

6   Thematic English

Current developments in language teaching in the primary school are based on the principle that language is integral to everything a child does. Children learn about their world and about themselves by using language.

Various areas of language — listening, speaking, reading and writing — are now seen within the context of the child's total development. Individual children's needs and interests are the basis of a unified language programme. Thus English is not seen as a 'subject', but as in integral part of the whole school curriculum in which *the child* is the primary consideration.

Teachers are trying to find ways of bringing together diverse English activities to result in a satisfying total achievement. Various 'thematic' or 'experience' approaches are being used. The provision of a stimulating classroom environment — a combination of materials, situation and atmosphere — is important, so that children can develop language through experience.

The following programmes are based on the idea of the development of language and creativity without subject barriers. *Reading* has an important place in the schemes listed here. (Many more thematic programmes, giving emphasis to other aspects of language, are available.)

Resources

Group Activity Topics (Nelson).
Language Stimulus Programme (Nelson).
Workshop of Ideas (Cassell).
Penguin Primary Project (Penguin Education).
Ideas Series: Bright Ideas, Young Ideas, More Ideas (Macmillan).
Language and How to Use It (Scott Foresman).
Language Development Programme for Primary Schools (Blackie).

Thematic Reading Guides

Puffins, Projects and Primary Schools. Penguin; *Penguinways.*

Children's Books for Junior Libraries: fiction and non-fiction, Junior Books Ltd, Earls Road, Grangemouth, Stirlingshire FK3 8XE.

P. Clarke, *Natural Science;* J. Adweth, *The World in Stories;* R. Colebourn, *The Greek and Roman World* — selected book lists, SLA, Victoria House, 29-31 George Street, Oxford OX1 2AY.

Further Reading

G. Pappas, *Reading in the Primary School* (Macmillan).

P.Rance, *Teaching by Topics* (Ward Lock Educational).

S.M. Lane and M. Kemp, *An Approach to Creative Writing in the Primary School* (Blackie).

7 Developing a School Reading Programme

A. Sequential Reading Schemes

In order to ensure an effective programme, consideration must be given to both readability levels and usage areas. This will allow flexible placement of children according to skill development in reading, as well as to particular reading needs such as leisure reading, consolidation or supplementary reading.

Planning a Buying Programme

When considering the relative costs of reading schemes, there will be advantages in spending the same amount of money to buy *two* schemes which cater to different sensory areas or which vary in their emphases, rather than just to buy the one scheme. [1]

Before spending money on reading material, an evaluation of the needs of the school, classes and teachers must be made. Material already in the school can be listed. Study a chart giving readability levels and usage areas for books and make comparisons. This will indicate deficiencies, and form the basis for a purchasing programme.

It is essential that basic teaching materials are available in multiple copies to enable effective group instruction. Consider the grouping of children within each grade, and the rostering and timetabling needed for maximum use of books and materials.

When purchasing new schemes it is important to be acquainted with their basic structure and to understand the authors' aims and principles. These must be in line with school educational policy and the beliefs of the teachers who will use them.

APPLICATION OF MATERIAL
RESOURCES WITHIN A SCHOOL

EVALUATION OF THE PRESENT
SITUATION

There are many ways of planning a
reading programme within a school.
Much of the programme will depend on
factors from several of these areas.

NEEDS School Teachers Children	Objectives	Short term Long term
	Special Consideration	Sequential Independent Remedial
COST	Availability of money	Planned buying
ENTHUSIASM	Teachers (Methods used)	
PRACTICALITY	Facilities	Materials Library
	Physical aspects Timetabling	
CONTROL	Testing Retesting Recording	

Whatever the operatives, the programme
must be evaluated on its effectiveness
in equipping children with better reading
skills than those they had before
their involvement in the programme.
*The material is only an aid to the
teaching of reading and makes it
easier for the teacher to teach;
effective results depend upon its
effective use.* Much material is
abused through misuse.

Guide to Usage Classification

Four main usage areas should be considered:

Basic Teaching Series
There are two broad types:
Interest Age is parallel to Reading Age, e.g. *Time for Reading* (Ginn)
Interest Age is higher than Reading Age (remedial type) e.g. *Adventures in Reading Series* (OUP)

Consolidation
There are two broad types:
Banded —   e.g. *Dolphin Books* (Hodder and Stoughton)
Sequential — e.g. *Look Ahead* (Heinemann)

Specific Skills
These incorporate skill areas such as word usage and comprehension. They are designed to complement the basic programme, e.g. *Sound Sense* (E.J. Arnold)

Enrichment
Books for leisure/pleasure reading (well-written books), e.g. *Gazelle, Antelope* and *Reindeer Series* (Hamish Hamilton); *Picture Puffin, Young Puffin* and *Puffin* Books (Penguin)

Guide to Readability Classification

Many sources of information are a guide only, and teacher evaluation in the light of school needs often has bearing on a book's placement as far as both readability level and usage area is concerned.
1. Reading charts and lists:
    Puffins, Projects and Primary Schools; Penguinways (Penguin Books, Harmondsworth, Middlesex).
    Children's Books for Junior Libraries; fiction and non-fiction (Junior Books Ltd, Earls Road, Grangemouth, Stirlingshire FK3 8XE).
    P. Clarke, *Natural Science;* J. Adcock, *The World in Stories;* R. Colebourn, *The Greek and Roman World* — selected book lists (SLA, Victoria House, 29-31 George Street, Oxford OX1 2AY).

B. Raban and W. Body, *Books for Reluctant Readers;*
C. Moon, *Individualised Reading* (Centre for the Teaching of Reading, 29 Eastern Avenue, Reading RG1 5RU).
Atkinson, E. and Gains, C. *A-Z List of Reading and Subject Books;* R. Edwards, *A Supplement to Reading and Subject Books* (National Association for Remedial Education, 4 Oldcroft Road, Walton-on-the-Hill, Stafford ST17 0LF).
2. Handbooks and manuals to reading schemes.
3. Education Gazettes, reviews in professional journals, Curriculum and Research Bulletins.
4. *Books in Schools* (United Kingdom Reading Association).

B. Some Points for Consideration when Examining New Reading Schemes, Books and Apparatus[2]

Vera Southgate
School of Education, University of Manchester

The Teacher's Point of View

1. What are the teacher's basic beliefs abut children learning to read — 'incidental learning' or 'systematic teaching'?
2. What are the head teacher's beliefs and consequently the 'climate' of the school?
3. What is the classroom organization within which the teacher feels able to do the best work? Is it basically formal or informal? Will the reading approach fit into this framework?
4. Does the approach fit in with what the teacher believes about the ways in which children learn? For example, if it is true that a child learns by doing, does the approach afford children the opportunity of being active in the learning situation?
5. Does the teacher want to be always initiating the teaching and learning or does he want the scheme to encourage and cater for children working on their own?
6. Is the teacher looking for a complete basic reading scheme, an aid to an existing reading scheme or supplementary books?

7. Is the teacher looking for an approach which is basically look-and-say, basically phonic, or a combination of both; or is she looking for a new idea for simplifying the intitial difficulties arising from the inconsistencies of our written language?
8. Does the teacher prefer written work to be incorporated in the scheme or not?
9. What is the range of reading attainments which the teacher is expecting the scheme to cater for?
10. How much will the new approach cost? (This figure requires working out in detail for each separate class, according to the various needs of the children in the class.)

The Needs of the Children

1. Number of children in the class.
2. Age range.
3. Intelligence.
4. Reading attainments.
5. Home backgrounds and interests.
6. Special problems of failing readers.

The Author's Ideas

1. Read carefully the teacher's manual, or the instructions.
2. Are the author's basic beliefs and aims in line with the teacher's?
3. Alternatively, does the scheme or approach fulfil a need which the teacher has previously felt but perhaps not defined?
4. Consider the background of the originator of the scheme; for example, he may have had experience as a teacher of infants, juniors, illiterate adolescents or adults, or educationally sub-normal children. If your pupils are not in the same age group, has the author applied his principles successfully to the age group and category of children you are teaching? If the author is not a teacher, but perhaps an educationist, a psychologist or a linguist, have his ideas been tried out in practical situations and have his ideas been applied successfully to the age of children with whom you are concerned?

The Books or Schemes

1. Consider the presentation, interest, illustrations, vocabulary, print, length, size and durability of reading books.
2. In look-and-say schemes, consider the vocabulary control in two ways:
   a) gradient of introduction of new words;
   b) the frequency of repetition of words.
3. In look-and-say schemes, is there an abundance of suitable supplementary material?
4. In phonic schemes consider:
   a) the steepness of gradient in the introduction of rules;
   b) the opportunities for practising the rules, particularly in interesting and different situations;
   c) the opportunities for transferring the skills which are being acquired.
5. Purchase the whole scheme, i.e. all the supplementary books and all the apparatus.
6. In the first instance, use the scheme as the author intended it to be used. (Until the teacher is thoroughly familiar with a scheme, it is unlikely that the innovations or deletions which he makes to a carefully planned reading programme will be in the nature of improvements.)

Apparatus

The selection of reading apparatus poses special difficulties for the teacher. In addition to the following guide, many of the earlier points in this section are relevant to the selection of apparatus.

1. Is there a teacher's manual or pamphlet which states precisely the author's aims in the production of the apparatus? (Odd pieces of apparatus are rarely valuable.)
2. Is the apparatus intended as a complete scheme or as a supplement to other schemes?
3. If it is not complete in itself, does it really supplement the other work in reading which will be going on in the classroom?
4. Are there careful and detailed instructions to the teacher for using the apparatus?

5. Are the rules which the children must follow simple and clear?
6. Will the children actually learn something from using this apparatus or will it just occupy them? (The teacher needs to ask himself this question at each stage.)
7. Will it take a large amount of the teacher's time to prepare the apparatus in the first instance, and then to arrange storage for it and organize it for each lesson?
8. Alternatively, is the apparatus designed so that the children can put out and generally take care of it and be in charge of it?
9. Is the apparatus attractive and durable?
10. Is the apparatus self-checking in some way, or will the children complete the task in a minute or two and then have to wait twenty minutes for the teacher to check it?
11. How many children does one set of apparatus cater for?
12. What will it cost to provide the apparatus for the class or group which is going to use it?

C. Further Notes on Evaluation of Basic Reading Schemes

Some infant teachers, bored by the dreariness of traditional readers and alarmed that many children fail to learn to read, are rejecting some of the well known readers with their limited, highly controlled vocabularies, and selecting attractive high-interest materials which engage the children's attention, encourage identification and provide greater challenge and stimulation. These are the main criticisms of some traditional readers:

1. Vocabulary Control

Limiting and simplifying to the degree seen in the initial readers of some reading schemes presents a barrier to understanding because *the language of readers is not the language that children normally use.* The following is a good test of the content of a reader: cover the illustrations and read it through; does it make good sense as a story? Do you recognize the natural speech patterns of children? The initial books of some schemes have little story li.ne, and this makes the text incoherent. Adventure, suspense and humour are rare. *The child finds that reading is not a meaningful activity.*

We all know how important it is to ensure that children know the difference between left and right before they begin reading, don't we? Left to go it alone, many of them will start somewhere in the middle of the sentence — even begin with the word at the end. We have been told often enough that dear old *Janet and John* needed bringing up-to-date, but I didn't realize how radical a face-lift it may require until last week. A reading expert pointed out that with a sentence like, 'Look, John, look', you might just as well start at the end and work backwards anyway. [3]

2. Illustrations Should Give Meaningful Clues

When texts are artificial and banal the illustrations often do not give clues to the sense. They may even distract the child.

3. Identification

Many children cannot recognize the prim stereotyped characters in some readers. They cannot identify with their activities or their environment.

An ideal reading scheme with any pretensions to educational power and efficiency would have to come to terms with cultural, environmental, social, sexual and — these days — racial factors. This is simply to say that it should come to terms with life' as it really is, and cease to reflect the wilfully prim and irrelevant world of Janet and John and Dick and Dora, who bore the children and grate on the teachers. [4]

4. Girls and Women are 'Inferior' in School Texts

Text books and general reading material used in schools often reflect the negative and passive roles of women in society. A conference on 'Women in Sexist Education' found that infant school readers and children's picture books have stories in which men, boys and male animals predominate. Those females who do feature are portrayed in 'stereotyped' roles, and adult females, human and animal, are invariably drawn wearing aprons.

In Sweden, school texts are being re-written to exclude discrimination and stereotyping of a sexist nature. We can choose those that discriminate least.

Below is a checklist of principles to assist in the selection of reading schemes:

☐ The text should be written in a variety of high quality literary styles, but framed in a linguistic structure that is commensurate with the linguistic development of the 'average' child at his appropriate reading level. Moreover, the language used should be naturalistic and present phonological elements that are neutral in that they do not favour one dialect over another.

☐ A balance should be achieved, in terms of content, between the local environment and a variety of different cultural environments.

☐ The structure of the series should enable the teacher to provide reading activities that are suitable to each child's intellectual and emotional development. This, in effect, means that the teacher will teach children rather than teach the material to the children. In addition, there should be opportunities for the children to work together in group and class activities.

☐ The series should provide a wide range of experiences ˙ which serve as stimuli for excursions into other language arts activities. At the same time the teacher must be permitted to incorporate spontaneous occurrences into reading lessons, which means that the suggested learning experiences should be open-ended.

☐ A sequential series of reading skills, covering language, perception, word attack, comprehension and study skills, should be developed. This means the involvement of all modalities in the learning process.

☐ The series should include the research findings relating to the physical presentation of reading materials and be illustrated in such a way as to present attractive stimuli to children.

☐ Sufficient guidance to assist teachers with classroom management should be provided but not at the expense of robbing the teacher of her own initiative.

☐ Above all, the series should develop a positive attitude to reading and enable the children to discover that learning to read is an enjoyable process.

Recording Reading Progress

Some kind of record should be kept of children's progress through the sequential reading programme:
☐ Vertically through achievement levels;
☐ Horizontally — consolidation reading for mastery.
As soon as they are able, children can record the books they read.

A record is useful when a teacher takes over a class during the year, and when children have moved to a new class in the new school year.

N.B. While a multi-level sequential reading programme is useful in junior primary years, it can be unnecessarily restrictive in senior years, especially for independent readers, limiting their range of reading. While common texts or basic books can be studied, a wide variety of books should be available.
See George Pappas, *Reading in the Primary School* (Macmillan).
See also Appreciation sections, p.77 and p.80 in this book.

There is no need to feel that one cannot help people learn to read without a lot of expensive material. Use what you have, take what you can get, and make what you need. [5]

D. Interest-Based Reading [6]
Don Tyrer

How often have you taken your class out for a walk to some local place of interest — a river, a lake, a park or a factory? Both you and the children were excited about being out of your room. You went to the river hoping to initiate a whole variety of experiences — pollution, fishing, frogs, rusting, water flow and not least the opportunity to develop a social feeling within the group. All of your hopes were fulfilled: the children caught frogs, collected rusty cans, everyone has a jar of dirty water, most were soaking wet to the knees. The whole experience brought the group closer together and initiated a host of possibilities; the children were talkative comparing their catches, enthusiasm was high.

Reading can have the same excitement as a walk to the river but why have we loaded our schools with reading schemes designed to teach children but which have nothing in them about frogs and falling in rivers? Admittedly there are some new sequential schemes which have attempted to cater for children's interests, but the problem is that by the time the children are up to the story on frogs they are interested in something else. We seem to have lost our sense of perspective about reading. Reading must be fun, exciting and directly about children's experiences so that the author and child share an experience. We have concentrated our efforts on the mechanics of being able to read (and children must learn the mechanics), but we have neglected the absolute necessity of children seeing the need for and feeling the joys of reading.

A number of people have become interested in the relationship of motivation to learning in the field of reading. Here is what a few of them have had to say —

A child will learn to read when he sees some point in the activity. [7]

He is disadvantaged if he is poor, but he may be impoverished and be rich. He is impoverished if he does not read with pleasure, because if he does not read with pleasure he is unlikely to read at all. [8]

Children cannot learn to hate and fear the printed word without being taught to do so. [9]

How then can we as teachers both teach children the skills of reading and have children see for themselves the value of these skills? One way is to incorporate with your individual skills programme an interest-based reading scheme. Interest-based reading is just one method of organizing books so that children can choose to read stimulating books appropriate to their interests and ability. It is not a method of teaching reading but of organization of material so that teachers can work through their children's interests with the minimum of difficulty.

Teachers who base their reading programmes on a language experience approach would find interest-based reading very helpful. Teachers who prefer using a sequential scheme may find interest-based reading to be a very good method of organizing the consolidation and enrichment sections of their schemes.

Organization

Interest-based reading organizes books under two criteria:
1. Broad reading-age levels;
2. Interest topics.

1. Broad Reading-age Levels

The method proposed is to divide books into five levels:

Level	Approximate reading age
A	5.0 — 6.0 years
B	6.0 — 7.6 years
C	7.6 — 8.6 years
D	8.6 — 10.0 years
E	10.0 — 11.6 years

2. Interest Topics

Having placed books into broad reading-age levels each level is then sub-divided into topics.

Having organized the books under these two criteria they are put in cardboard or wooden boxes, with the front of the box colour coded for each level and labelled with the topic.

As each reading-age level is designated a separate colour it is advisable to label each book with an appropriate colour tag.

The final result is a series of boxes at each level arranged around the suggested topics.

Teachers are then able to borrow boxes of books on any topic and from any level, take them to their rooms and use them in a variety of ways. Some schools allow children to borrow books directly from an interest-based scheme rather than the teacher taking boxes to their rooms.

Whatever method one uses to teach reading it is imperative that children experience reading as a rewarding and stimulating activity.

School libraries and interest-based reading schemes complement each other as the interest-based scheme provides classroom teachers with immediate access to boxes of books to be used in the classroom. The school library is an extension of the classroom and the place where children borrow books which are extensions of individual or classroom interests. The central library is a very valuable and necessary part of any school and interest-based reading schemes do not detract from their importance.

Interest-based reading stresses the need for children to be involved in the reading programme. It also recognizes that it is the teacher, rather than the teaching method used, which is paramount to the success of children learning to read.

E. Using the Fry Readability Formula
Peter Edwards

'Readability' is a term used to refer to the measurement of the approximate level of difficulty of written material.

Factors such as vocabulary, grammatical and concept complexity combine with format, typography, visual aids and the writer's style and organization to increase difficulty level. Formulas based on variables related to such factors have been developed for use in estimating difficulty. Aukerman (1972) described a readability formula as '. . . an objective method of measuring several components of writing which, when considered in relation to each other, result in a quantitative estimate of the reading difficulty of the sample.'

The works of Bormuth (1966, 1972) provide the best analysis of the state-of-art in readability research. Some readability formulas use eight or more variables. Out of the plethora of those published, the most effective have consistently restricted themselves to two, or at most, three variables. Two of the most widely used are the Spache (1953) formula for junior levels and the Dale-Chall (1948) formula for secondary levels. Both formulas are complex and require considerable computation time. For example, it takes approximately one hour of computation time for each sample used in applying the Dale-Chall formula if you have some practice in using the word list. It must be emphasized that readability formulas are still in the developmental state and by no means solve all the problems in estimating difficulty of material. The formulas are not totally accurate, usually estimating the difficulty of the material within a year or two. (There is, of course, no such thing as a totally accurate estimate of the true difficulty of printed material.) The formulas are the best tools now available to us; the results are quite useful in estimating difficulty when supported by subjective analysis of other factors. Used in conjunction with teacher judgement and a knowledge of the interests and abilities of students at a particular age level, the formulas can provide valuable insight into the difficulty of printed material. Teacher judgement of the interests and abilities of students is a matter of professional development and comes with practice in the schools.

The Fry (1968) formula is a recently developed technique which has been widely used by researchers and teachers. The formula uses average sentence length and average number of syllables in the aggregate of three 100-word samples. These averages are then plotted on a graph to give the readability age level of the reading material.

The Fry formula purports to give an age level which represents general understanding (75%) by the reader of the printed material. It is a technique which is being effectively used by both primary and secondary school teachers. There follows a description of the Fry formula and use of the Fry Readability Graph.

Directions for Working the Readability Graph

1. Randomly select three sample passages and count out exactly one hundred words. Start at the beginning of a sentence. Don't count numbers. Do count proper nouns.
2. Count the number of sentences in the hundred words estimating length of the fraction of the last sentence to the nearest 1/10th.
3. Count the total number of syllables in the hundred-word passage. If you don't have a hand counter available, an easy way is to simply put a mark above every syllable over one in each word, then when you get to the end of the passage, count the number of marks and add one hundred.
4. Enter graph with average sentence length and number of syllables; plot dot where the two lines intersect. Area where dot is plotted will give you the approximate grade level.
5. If a great deal of variability is found, putting more sample counts into the average is desirable. Few books will fall in the grey area but when they do, grade level scores are invalid.

Example:

	syllables	*sentences*
1st hundred words	124	6.6
2nd hundred words	141	5.5
3rd hundred words	158	6.8
Average	141	6.3

Graph for Estimating Readability
by Edward Fry, Rutgers University Reading Centre, New Jersey

The graph below refers to grade levels in the United States. Reading age is equivalent to the grade level plus 5. E.g. grade 7 is equivalent to reading age 12 years.

The dot plotted on the graph indicates 7th grade readability.

Average number of syllables per 100 words

SHORT WORDS   LONG WORDS

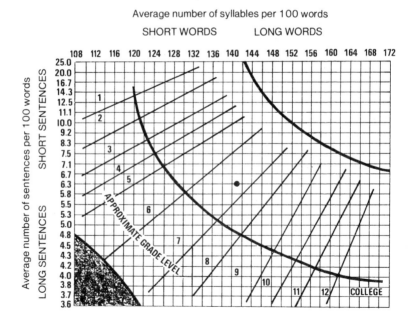

Further Reading

D.R. Aukerman, *Reading in the Secondary School Classroom* (McGraw-Hill).

John R. Bormuth, 'Readability: A New Approach', *Reading Research Quarterly*, 1 (1966), pp. 79-131.

Edgar Dale and Jeanne S. Chall, 'A Formula for Predicting Readability', *Educational Research Bulletin*, 27 (1948), pp. 11-21.

Edward Fry, 'A Readability Formula That Saves Time', *Journal of Reading*, 11 (April, 1968), pp. 513-6, 575-8.

George D. Spache, 'A New Readability Formula for Primary Grade Reading Materials', *Elementary School Journal*, 53 (March, 1953), pp. 410-13.

J. Gilliland, *Readability* (Hodder and Stoughton, 2nd edn)

G.R. Klare, *The Measurement of Readability* (Iowa State University Press).

8 Testing

Attainment Testing — Although the depth of its interpretation must necessarily be limited, the comprehension-type group reading test is a valuable initial screening device. Its indication of relative levels of achievement — dependence, independence, etc. — opens avenues for further investigation into skill development.

Diagnostic Testing — Comparative measures of sight vocabulary and word-attack skills may be gained with a *word identification test.* As well as being a useful indicator of skill strengths and weaknesses in the dependent stage, it is a guide to appropriate leisure reading and classroom-working levels of children at a stage of semi-independence.

Word-attack skill weaknesses, evident from performance on a word identification test, may be investigated more with a *phonic elements test.* Specific disabilities and possible starting points for remedial instruction will be indicated.

Children's sight vocabularies may be matched precisely with specific reading series through reference to *sequential word lists* taken directly from the reading series.

Attainment test — will give a general indication of levels of skill development within a year group.

Word identification test — is likely to be applicable to those within this area of the distribution.

Phonic elements test — should be applied *as needed* as a follow-up to the word identification — not to all at this level.

A. Nature and Uses of Standardized Attainment Tests

Attainment tests — also known as achievement tests or more loosely as comprehension tests — are usually given to a whole class or a group of children at the same time. They can of course be given individually. A standardized achievement test is a carefully constructed instrument with certain characteristics.

Scientific methods have been used in the

☐ selection of items;

☐ discriminative value of the items;

☐ standarization procedures.

Attainment tests are designed to sample single aspects of skill areas of the complexity of the reading process.

The result of any test should be regarded as a measure of the aspect tested and not a measure of the overall subject.

Teachers should predetermine the test best suited to measure the area under question and that most appropriate to the range of abilities in their class.

Tests are designed either as group or individual tests.

Group attainment tests are *time saving* as large numbers of children can be tested at the same time.

Individual attainment tests are *time consuming* where large numbers are concerned, but they provide opportunities for a more sensitive and qualitatively valuable assessment of the individual.

Use of Standardized Attainment Tests

Used wisely, with due regard to their limitations, attainment tests may do the following:

☐ *Sort and rank* the year group to allow more effective group and/or individual teaching.

☐ *Indicate general strengths or weaknesses* in the aspect tested.

☐ *Indicate a need for more specific testing* in the form of attainment and/or diagnostic testing.

☐ *Give an indication for teaching* in a developmental programme.

☐ *Assist the teacher* in the evaluation and re-evaluation of his teaching.

Attainment tests should not be used as a labelling device.

A child's test result may vary from test to test and from day to day. Emotions, physical health and the influence of environment may affect a child's performance. Qualitative observations in the test situation, background knowledge of the children and other information available to the teacher can be of value in interpreting test results. *Teachers should be flexible and sensitive in their interpretation of the test results. The teacher knows the child — the test does not.*

The attainment tests should be regarded as only the beginning to a teaching programme or the re-evaluation of the existing programme.

Do not over-test in any one year.

Administration Procedures for Standardized Tests

1. Read the manual *carefully* and be familiar with the purpose and range of expectations of the test. Be sure it is the test you need!
2. Be *sincere* and *sensitive* in *all* test situations.
3. Before administration:
   a) Seating arrangement of the children: seek the co-operation of another teacher to take half the class so that there is one child to a desk; all pens, rulers, rubbers and books placed on the desk.
   b) Have spare pencils ready.
   c) If a timed test, have stop watch or watch with second hand.
   d) If an untimed test, arrange work to occupy the child who finishes early.
   e) Clear the blackboard for test instructions.
   f) Prepare blackboard instructions when needed.
   g) Take into account most suitable time of day — preferably mornings.
   h) Place a notice on the door e.g. *'Do not enter. Testing in progress.'*
   i) Prepare a rough draft of the instructions. It is essential to ensure correct procedure.
4. Interruptions during test *must be avoided.*
5. Establish rapport to provide for maximum effort.
6. The tester should: be friendly and encouraging throughout the duration of the test situation; not indicate a difficult situation; *adhere strictly to test instructions and time as prescribed in the manual.*
7. The tester must *test* and not *teach.*
8. The tester should observe qualitative aspects of the test.

9. Correction:
   a)   correct accurately according to instructions;
   b)   sensitivity but consistency in correction is important.

B. *Diagnostic Testing*

As distinct from an attainment test, a diagnostic reading test is a testing-searching device aimed at *discovering,* rather than *measuring,* the specific weaknesses in development of skill areas.

Diagnosis by definition is:
A careful and detailed study by examination of the facts about something to find out its essential features, faults, strengths, etc.

Diagnostic test material is selected to provide a basis for examining the sequence of the steps of elements involved in the learning process under consideration.

It is the tester's responsbility to be sufficiently well-informed of the skills involved in learning to read to be able to select the appropriate tests for securing the diagnostic information sought.

The tester must become familiar with the administration procedures of any test to be used and then be sure to adhere to the instructions provided.

When interpreting results, the teacher needs to be sensitive to the child's progress, his emotional reaction and the possibility that the child may become weary or frustrated. In the hands of the sensitive teacher, the diagnostic test may indicate specific *strengths* and *weaknesses* and will frequently give an indication of the areas in which teaching emphasis is required.

Tests

Standard Reading Tests (Daniels & Diack Battery) —
   Comprehensive battery of diagnostic tests (Hart-Davis).
Gates-McKillop Reading Diagnostic Tests (Teachers College
   Press, New York).
Doren Diagnostic Test of Word Recognition Skills (American

Guidance Service; Educational Enterprises, Bristol act as agents).

Neale Analysis of Reading Ability — Forms *A*, *B*, and *C* (Macmillan).

The Edwards Reading Test (Heinemann Educational).

See also *Reading: Tests and Assessment Techniques*, P.D. Pumfrey (Hodder and Stoughton).

C. The Role of the Class Teacher

Teachers should have the opportunity to become familiar with the usage, administration, and interpretation of selected Attainment and Diagnostic Tests and to gain some knowledge of additional tests that may also be of value to them.

Name of test	Type of test	Age range	Time needed to do the test	Areas sampled
Doren Diagnostic Reading Test (American Guidance Service: Educational Enterprises, Bristol act as agents)	A group or individual diagnostic test	6-15 years	Approx. 3 hours for the whole test	1. Knowledge of letter names and sounds 2. Word recognition 3. Auditory discrimination 4. Blending 5. Rhyming 6. Vowel sounds
Gates — McKillop Reading Diagnostic Tests (Teachers College Press, New York)	An individual diagnostic test	8-12 years	Approx. 3-4 hours for the whole test (but separate sub-tests can be given)	1. Oral reading 2. Word recognition 3. Knowledge of letter names and sounds 4. Blending 5. Vowel sounds 6. Spelling and vocabulary 7. Syllabification 8. Auditory discrimination
Daniels & Diack Test 12 — Graded Test of Reading Experience (Chatto and Windus)	A group attainment test	6-14 years	Approx. 20-30 minutes	1. Silent reading 2. Literal comprehension
Schonell's Test R3 — Reading Test 4 (Oliver and Boyd)	A group attainment test	7-11 years	Exactly 9 minutes (a timed test)	1. Silent reading 2. Literal comprehension

Name of test	Type of test	Age range	Time needed to do the test	Areas sampled
Schonell's Test R4 — Silent Reading Test B (Oliver and Boyd)	A group attainment test	9-13 years	Exactly 15 minutes (a timed test)	1. Silent reading 2. Literal comprehension
The GAP Test (Heinemann Educational)	A group attainment test	8-12 years	Approx. 15 minutes	Comprehension (using the cloze technique)
The Neale Analysis of Reading Ability (Macmillan)	An individual attainment test, which is also partially diagnostic Forms A, B and C	6-12 years	Approx. 10-15 minutes	1. Oral reading 2. Literal oral comprehension 3. Blending) small Spelling) supplementary Phonics) tests
Daniels & Diack Test 1 — The Standard Test of Reading Skill (All Daniels & Diack Tests listed below are published by Hart-Davis)	An individual attainment test	5-9 years	Approx. 10-20 minutes	1. Oral reading 2. Literal comprehension
Schonell's Test R1 — The Graded Reading Vocabulary Test (All Schonell's Tests listed below are published by Oliver and Boyd)	An individual attainment test	5-15 years	Approx. 5-10 minutes	Oral word recognition (graded ability)

Schonell's Test R2 — Simple Prose Reading Test	An individual attainment test	6-9 years	Approx. 15 minutes	1. Oral reading 2. Literal comprehension
Daniels & Diack Test 2 — Copying Abstract Figures	A group or individual test	5-9 years	Approx. 5-10 minutes	Visual-motor co-ordination
Daniels & Diack Test 3 — Copying a Sentence	A group or individual diagnostic test	5-9 years	Approx. 5 minutes	Visual-motor co-ordination
Daniels & Diack Test 4 — Visual Discrimination and Orientation Test	An individual diagnostic test	5-9 years	Approx. 5-10 minutes	1. Visual discrimination 2. Left-right orientation
Daniels & Diack Test 5 — Letter Recognition Test	An individual diagnostic test	5-9 years	Approx. 10 minutes	1. Knowledge of letter names and sounds 2. Visual discrimination 3. Auditory discrimination
Daniels & Diack Test 6 — Aural Discrimination	An individual diagnostic test	5-9 years	Approx. 10 minutes	1. Visual discrimination 2. Auditory discrimination
Daniels & Diack Test 7A — Word-Recognition Test	An individual diagnostic test	5-9 years	Approx. 5 minutes	Word recognition of 2 and 3 letter words
Daniels & Diack Test 7B — Word-Recognition Test	An individual diagnostic test	5-9 years	Approx. 5 minutes	Initial consonant blending
Daniels & Diack Test 7H — Word-Recognition Test	An individual diagnostic test	5-9 years	Approx. 5 minutes	Oral reading of nonsense syllables

Name of test	Type of test	Age range	Time needed to do the test	Areas sampled
Daniels & Diack Test 8 — Oral Word-Recognition Test	An individual diagnostic test	5-9 years	Approx. 10 minutes	1. Visual discrimination 2. Auditory discrimination
Daniels & Diack Test 9 — Picture-Word Recognition	An individual diagnostic test	5-9 years	Approx 10-15 minutes	Visual discrimination
Daniels & Diack Test 10 — Silent Prose — Reading and Comprehension Test	An individual diagnostic test	5-9 years	Approx. 15 minutes	1. Silent reading 2. Literal comprehension
Schonell's Test R5 — A Test of Analysis and Synthesis of Words Containing Common Phonic Units	An individual diagnostic test	5-13 years	Approx. 5-10 minutes	Oral word recognition, involving words to test phonics, syllabification, blending (indirectly and word attack)
Schonell's Test R6 — A Test of Directional Attack on Words	An individual diagnostic test	5-13 years	Approx. 5 minutes	Oral word recognition, involving words to test partial and full reversals
Schonell's Test R7 — Visual Word Discrimination Test	An individual diagnostic test	5-13 years	Approx. 15-20 minutes	Visual discrimination
Daniels & Diack Test 7C — Word-Recognition Test	An individual diagnostic test	5-9 years	Approx. 5 minutes	Final consonant blending

Daniels & Diack Test 7D — Word-Recognition Test	An individual diagnostic test	5-9 years	Approx. 5 minutes	Syllabification
Daniels & Diack Test 7E — Word-Recognition Test	An individual diagnostic test	5-9 years	Approx. 10 minutes	Word recognition, using words to test blending, phonics and silent *e*
Daniels & Diack Test 7F — Word-Recognition Test	An individual diagnostic test	5-9 years	Approx 5 minutes	Oral word recognition (words of irregular spelling)
Daniels & Diack Test 7G — Word-Recognition Test	An individual diagnostic test	5-9 years	Approx. 5 minutes	Oral word recognition (reversible words)

9 Research and Opinion

Evaluation in Reading[1]
D.J. Ryan and M. Savage

Reading is a special facet of human activity that can be impaired by the mis-use of tests. This paper is an unashamed attack on the pedagogical malpractices that derive from testing in the area of reading. Many so-called reading tests do not measure reading ability at all. They are at odds with what is now known about the reading process.

On the positive side, this paper at least touches on what is involved in the reading process. It suggests how we might approach evaluation of the way an individual performs in a reading task. It points out the need to establish clearly defined goals for a reading programme if evaluation in this area is to be effective. It should undoubtedly help those wishing to formulate the objectives for reading instruction.

The ideas contained in this paper stem from the authors' research, reading and discussion on the topic. Readers interested in pursuing the sources of inspiration might care to read the following:

F. Smith, *Reading,* CUP, 1978.
F. Smith, *Understanding Reading,* New York; Holt, Rinehart and Winston, 1971.
F. Smith, *Psycholinguistics and Reading,* New York; Holt, Rinehart and Winston, 2nd edn 1973.
K.S. Goodman, (ed.) *The Psycholinguistic Nature of the Reading Process,* Detroit; Wayne State University Press, 1968.

Should we tell children that their language abilities are poor in areas such as listening, speaking or writing? It may be unwise to dub children with any label designating a particular level of language competence. On the other hand, it may conceivably do some good to some children, provided that assessment of competence in such language areas is valid. It would be professionally irresponsible to act this way if there was uncertainty about the nature of the assessment made. It seems easy to judge whether or not a person is skilful in the use of language but it is a most difficult thing to measure these skills in quantitative terms. If reading is the most complex linguistic process undertaken by children, and a good case can be made out to show that it is, then the evaluation of ability in this sphere should be regarded at least as tentatively as that in any other area of verbal communication. Yet we put great faith in the various reading tests commonly used. We grade children and often disregard the attitudes to reading this procedure develops in them. We isolate the failures and usually ignore the arbitrary basis of our decisions in allotting them to remedial groups — and our problems in reading remain.

There is no evidence to show that increasing involvement by teachers and schools with testing programmes has brought any improvement in the reading environment for children. But it has led, amongst teachers, to a dependence on standardized tests that is unhealthy where insufficient consideration is given to the nature of the information obtained. Where scores are so crudely determined, important pedagogical decisions should be made with great caution. A finding like 'three months retarded in reading' has a veneer of precision but without other evidence it is a piece of educationally worthless information. Such findings are often grossly misleading and never adequate for teachers wishing to assess competence among their pupils.

Educational Value

Tests in reading should not be to the educational disadvantage of children. We should ask what benefit the test will be to the child before he attempts it. Achievement tests as used at present are commonly of little, if any, value to children as far as the development of reading ability is concerned. This is inevitable because these tests are based on assumptions of such doubtful validity. It is quite wrong to say that:

(i) Test results give direct measures of reading ability rather than some other skill;

(ii) All children do their best on reading tests;

(iii) The process of reading can be simply defined and, as a result, a simple sequence of development, identical for all children, exists in reading.

There is no clearly defined relationship between the development of perceptual skills, learning styles, cognitive abilities, age, maturity and experience. It is therefore not possible to measure a child's level of ability in reading as though it were a linear progression and obtain an accurate index of reading competence in the form of a discrete score. Clearly, if reading is a creative activity involving an active response, and is dependent on motivation, attitudes and experience, children will vary in the way they approach the task. The performance of some will reflect a broad encounter with the content of the text. That of others will reflect an attempt to apply a set of formally acquired skills. It could be said that because reading ability is so complex a phenomenon, 'achievement tests' will measure no more than a small aspect of this ability and will provide no delineation for a particular child of whatever component of reading ability is being tapped.

The Purposes of Testing

There are currently widespread demands on teachers to produce data on their pupils in the form of test results.

Reasons teachers give for using the various tests include:

(i) Grading children.

(ii) Reporting their level of attainment.

(iii) Diagnosing weaknesses.

The value of grading children in terms of reading ages and trying to match them with appropriate reading matter is seriously open to question:

a) There is no concensus among teachers or even among test constructors about the exact nature of reading ages and yet these are calculated and acted on as though they were precise quantities.

b) The criteria on which books are allotted to particular levels are not universally accepted and there is no general agreement about readability formulas. A child may find difficulty in reading a book because of word-recognition problems or even because he can raise no interest in the subject. He may find reading difficult because of the print size or the layout of the book or because of the complexity of the vocabulary, syntax or language style.

c) The assumption that children automatically benefit from being placed at their reading level (even if reading ability and readability could be accurately assessed) deserves to be strongly challenged.

There are often undesirable consequences of grading children in so obvious a way according to what is alleged to be their reading ability. The pressures generated which force children through 'colour levels' of reading schemes help focus attention on inconsequential aspects of reading programmes. Too often the recording associated with sequential reading schemes measures the quantity of printed matter processed by children but not the quality of reading.

Reading Ages

There is inordinate faith put in the concept of reading ages because they are regarded as the valid index of reading ability. Thus, a child whose reading age is less than his chronological age can be regarded as a failure. R.A. becomes just one more tag with the potential for acquiring an indelible character, and children tend to perform in accordance with expectations set for them.

In post-primary schools, a discrepancy between reading age and chronological age is often seen as the explanation for lack of success in almost any subject. Genuine distinctions are not made between inability to handle concepts on the one hand and reading disability on the other. The absence of motivation or interest, and the inappropriateness of study tasks are often ignored when the evidence from so-called reading tests is presented. Where children fail, reading becomes the scapegoat in a situation where a curriculum or teaching methods may not be adapting to cater for the needs of all children.

Reading ages are broad and global measures leave much information undisclosed. It cannot be doubted that there are children whose reading ages indicate satisfactory per-

formance but who lack skills necessary to guarantee efficiency in reading. The various tests commonly used give
different reading ages for any individual and it is thus a
dubious practice to base educational judgements on data so
ill-defined. Where correspondence between R.A. and C.A. is
regarded as the norm, the danger of aiming for just pass level
rather than excellence of performance need not be dwelt on.

1. Reading ages ignore the complex array of individual
   abilities that must be brought to bear on the reading task.
   Children are complex beings and reading is a complex
   process. Unless the total person and the total process are
   considered, reading will continue to be the problem area of
   the curriculum.

2. Children are tested to fulfil the requirements of reporting
   to other members of the school staff and to parents. Such
   reporting should be informative and indicative of progress
   over a given period of time, under stated conditions, and
   listing factors relating to interests, attitudes and
   difficulties. To report that a child does poorly in relation to
   other children in the class on comprehension exercises or
   has difficulty with word recognition skills is so general as to
   be useless. Numerical terms of colour codes may lead to the
   development of unwholesome attitudes among pupils and
   to repressive and recriminatory action by those who are to
   teach them.

3. Children are tested so that they can be allotted to remedial
   groups. If this concept is to be maintained, the tests used
   on which to base decisions about types of remediation
   should be better than rough screening tests. Many children
   in need of close personal attention are not detected under
   existing procedures.

A good starting point in diagnosing reading disability would
be to ask the child to define his reading problem, if any.

Constant screening over a wide range of areas is necessary
also. Any lag in the development of reading ability may
become discernible at times other than at initial screening
sessions. The effect of deprivations may similarly emerge at
any point in a child's school career.

The view is widely held that the best diagnostic tests now
used enable teachers to look at all the separate abilities used in
reading. Such a view is erroneous until it can be shown that

sub-tests do tap distinct and different skills and that the diagnostic profiles derived embrace the entire reading operation. Most available tests actually assess skills common to many areas. Visual perception is not exclusively related to reading; nor is word knowledge, verbal skills or ability to organize information. Furthermore, these functions do not comprise the totality of the reading process. Most tests measure only pre-conditions, by-products or outcomes of reading and should more appropriately be called recoding, linguistic, memory or intelligence tests.

Adequate diagnostic evaluation must take account of the reader's strengths and learning style as applied to the reading process, of his social and educational background and of his motivation, attitudes and purposes in reading.

Test users should judge a diagnostic test in the light of the following criteria:

a) Does it have a clearly formulated rationale?
b) Does the rationale derive from viable concepts about the nature of the reading process?
c) Do the sub-tests stem directly from the principles enunciated in the rationale?
d) Is the rationale adequately represented in the battery of sub-tests?

Limitations of Standardized Tests

The scope of what reading tests measure is limited because professional test constructors must tread the safe path of examining only what can reliably be measured. This becomes of serious concern when, as commonly happens, the tests become the determining factor in the formulation of objectives. The content of reading tests tends to frame teachers' views about children's reading, and success in these tests becomes the goal of reading programmes. Admittedly, many aspects of the reading process are difficult to measure but this does not excuse test constructors, whose product purports to assess reading ability, from the obligation of acknowledging that other vital components of reading ability exist. Some tests, for example, enable a teacher to derive a score for reading ability by reference to the accuracy with which a passage is read aloud. The errors can be counted accurately enough but unless one takes account of the quality of the errors and perceives that some are caused by sophisticated language operations stemming from a developing skill in reading one can be misled. Accuracy may mean outstanding proficiency or laborious recoding, word by word, to the exclusion of understanding skill. That is, the reader may even be understanding what he reads so well that he can translate it into his own language style or actually improve the language of the author. One child, for example, made the following intelligent 'mistakes' in reading.

'You said *that* it could be anything I like.' (an insertion)

'Now Henry', said Dad ^{one} evening, 'we are . . . (substitution)
                              that

'*The* other children at school laughed at him.' (an omission)

   Much testing centres on the ability of children to recognize words from a given list. It is presumed that the single score derived from performance of such a task is an accurate indicator of reading ability. But efficient word recognition arises from the ability of the child to identify words as units of meaning in a grammatical context. Reading is not repeated word recognition. It is a sequential operation in which memory and linguistic knowledge are involved. Word recognition tests commonly fail to discriminate between children who are masters of a mechanical matching skill acquired only as a result of constant drill, and children whose search for meaning leads them to recognize units of language. In other words, there are some children whose word recognition ability is unrelated to the acquisition of meaning and their ability lies in being able to match the sound but not the concept to the graphic symbol. There are even children who have learned to recite parrot-fashion the first dozen or so items in their word recognition tests.

Group Tests

Teachers often demand group tests that are inexpensive to obtain, simple to administer, easy to score, with proven reliability and validity and, if possible, with national norms provided. They find convenient a single numerical score which can be converted to a reading age so that the business of classifying children, grouping them and reporting to parents is made easy. But if it is considered feasible to administer only group tests then the question of priorities in teaching must be raised. If reading is a fundamental ability to be acquired, its skills must be well taught. If effective teaching in this area depends on effective evaluation we cannot ignore the imperfections of group tests, the sources of error related to the test situation and the extremely limited amount of information such tests provide.

All tests of reading should provide sufficient information for the teacher to be able to establish hypotheses about the nature of actual or potential weaknesses among new pupils. All tests of reading ability should be centred on the elements of the reading process. This includes the cognitive and linguistic insights that children must direct to the reading task and the perceptual and psycho-motor operations involved. These are the major constituents of reading and to ignore them in the interests of saving time is false economy. To listen to a child read and to reflect on the components of the reading process may best enable effective evaluation.

The Reading Process

If one wants to make a medical diagnosis one must keep in mind the various systems and functions of the human body (digestive, circulatory, neurological, etc.). Similarly, one must take account of the age, sex, build and previous medical history of the person concerned. Proper diagnosis will not be based only on a variable like pulse rate. To examine reading ability it is also necessary to avoid viewing in isolation one or other of the familiar discrete indices of performance. It is necessary to consider both the individual and the entire reading process.

Basically, a person in a reading situation must respond to a *variety* of cue systems that are grapho-phonic, semantic and syntactic in origin. This means that the process of reading demands active participation by the reader. Thus, for example, in a simple sentence like 'The batsman runs down the pitch' the reader uses a certain amount of his knowledge of sound-symbol correspondence. He gleans some information by the evoking of familiar sound patterns from his language. He will anticipate sequences in language-speech sound sequences. That is, he will not need to undertake phonic analysis of whole words or of the entire sentence. Some word sequences deriving from the grammatical construction or the meaning will also be anticipated. As isolated words, the meaning of 'runs' and 'pitch' would be ambiguous. But in the context of the sentence, a child with reasonable familiarity with spoken English should have no difficulty in setting up the correct expectancy about the role of these words even before he sees them. Unless he does attend to the sentence as an English utterance he may not recognize that 'runs' has a verb function and that 'pitch' has a noun function. That is, he must identify the syntactic structure of the sentence before he is able to attach the correct meaning to the words. There are, however, no available reading tests which adequately assess the reader's ability to apply his syntactic knowledge to the reading task for the purpose of constructing meanings.

Efficient readers must develop skill in recognizing when a word is a compound of other smaller words or meaning-bearing segments of words. Readers recreate meanings, in some cases, from their perception of word parts like *unrecognizable* and in other cases from complete words, phrases or sentences. The testing of comprehension usually ignores the multi-level operation by which understandings are formed. Comprehension is often seen as ability to note factual details, to store information in short term memory, to perceive general significance or to make inferences. Such tests provide little information about the levels at which misunderstandings occur.

Currently used comprehension tests do not discriminate between children whose difficulties are basically in functioning with:

    graphic symbols;

    syntactic complexities;

    the concepts involved; (i.e. there are children whose performance is limited by their vocabulary and who would probably perform in a similar way even if the material was read to them).

Evaluation in reading, therefore, must entail an examination of the way children operate on patterns of words — recognizing and relating, responding to word functions and syntactic structure and processing information in terms of concepts and ideas. It must focus on the specific aspects of the stimulus that the reader selectively perceives, how he interprets the information and integrates it into his background knowledge.

Principles of Evaluation

a) Scope

Evaluation in reading should concentrate on making judgements not merely on children's performances but on the entire reading programme. For example, we might formally consider the level of interaction between reading ability and the other school subjects. We might make appraisal of the applicability of aids and materials in various reading situations, the effectiveness of innovations in teaching techniques in the particular school situation, the variety of reading matter available for children, the frequency with which the book stock is added to to cater for the emergence of new interests among children, and the availability of professional reading matter on the subject within the school. In drawing inferences about the effectiveness and quality of teaching it is of course inadequate to base judgements on a blanket set of scores derived from a group test. Teaching skill will be reflected in the performance of children if this is measured by noting the advance made by each child over his previous performance in the direction of stated goals.

Evaluation should be a continuing activity and an integral part of the teaching programme. A longitudinal assessment of an individual or group of children will enable a composite picture of reading progress to be built up over a period of time so that teaching can be modified accordingly. A teacher's failure to perceive a child's misconceptions may permit the development of unsound habits in reading.

b) Environment

Whatever evaluation is done should not provide an occasion for the development of unfavourable attitudes to reading. Fear, frustration or embarrassment will sometimes culminate reading activities. Thus, a climate is created in which skills are acquired only under duress. The snowball effect where children progress because they experience success and self-confidence will then be destroyed. The best evaluation may take place in what is effectively a normal, unsupervised reading situation. In this way, one can limit the intrusion of variables like motivation and anxiety that prevent valid interpretation of performance.

Consideration should also be given to the type of material children are presented with when evaluation is carried out. If the passages are short and contrived or mere excerpts without an adequate context, the performance of a child may not reflect his normal reading ability. A child's reading of test material, whether standardized or not, will be quite a different matter from that same child's reading of material that he has chosen. Tasks imposed under stress and unrelated to usual purposes in reading may produce information of little value.

In this context, tests of speed of reading should be treated with caution because rate of reading is only meaningful if it relates to a defined level of comprehension. Such a level cannot be pre-determined for a reader. One cannot calculate the amount of comprehension that takes place when a person reads but only assess performance on a particular test. It would be absurd to equate the ability of two readers, one of whom reads twice as fast as the other but with only half the comprehension. To assess speed of reading one must first define reading and comprehension. This obligation is usually overlooked by those who construct tests in this area. The obligation to define terms precisely also exists for teachers who attempt intervention in the field of reading rate.

In any case, flexibility in speed of reading would appear to be the most desirable outcome of reading instruction. The ability of the student to adapt his reading rate to the demands of the material or to suit his own purposes should be the issue under appraisal.

Directions in Evaluation

Educational evaluation requires the prior establishment of goals for a teaching programme. Without adequately stated objectives, evaluation will be random and piecemeal. It is necessary to define goals as precisely as possible and ultimately to express them in terms of observable behaviour. But before this task is attempted it would be worthwhile to consider the value of reading in present times.

The written word plays a unique part in the preservation and communication of experience. Books are still indispensable for facilitating the storage and transmission of knowledge. If education aims at the betterment of mankind then the written word and books should be part of the child's world. Whatever betterment takes place does so as a result of the transfer of ideas and the impact of the language in which they are embedded. The evaluation of reading, therefore, should concern itself with the effectiveness with which children acquire ideas through their reading and with their response to the language. However, no two children's background and experience and language are the same. Thus, insightful and meaningful reading will produce a large variety of acceptable responses to the stimulus material. Viewed in this light, the appraisal of reading should be concerned with the quality of a person's response, the richness of his interpretation and the extent to which he profits from the material read.

Three major goals for the teaching of reading are proposed. The prime goal at all stages of a programme should be the development of good attitudes to reading. By this, we mean that the act of reading should be something the child wishes to engage in and from which he gains satisfaction and pleasure. In behavioural terms it means that the child will use the library voluntarily, that his search for information will automatically lead him to books, that some of his leisure time will be used in reading, that he will develop new interests through reading, that he will handle books with care and will want to own books himself. He should show in some overt way (talking, writing, reflecting, laughing, doing) that he has been affected by his reading. He should be willing to share information enthusiastically (expanding, re-telling, re-enacting, discussing) after he has read. Evaluation in this area requires ample, open-ended situations as part of the reading scene.

The child may, for example, be invited to paraphrase orally what he has read, to extrapolate to another situation, to imagine how the story might be continued or to comment on it in terms of the language used and the ingenuity or plausibility of the plot. These activities provide valuable occasions for the teacher to gauge the effect of a written message on pupils and to judge whether reading has been worthwhile from the child's point of view.

The second major goal of reading instruction is to have the child understand that reading is a quest for meaning.

He should perceive that reading is an aspect of the communication processes. It is one of the ways of obtaining information from another person. Its reward should derive ideally from success in the activity itself and not from the successful production of 'right' answers to 'comprehension' questions. If one considers that children have different language and experiential backgrounds it can be seen that the 'comprehension exercise' approach limits the scope of the child's response. Such tasks constrain a reader to react in a narrow way and will inevitably encourage him to read as if he were part of the triangle which includes himself, the author and the questioner.

Usually, some intermediary has constructed the question, interpreted the author's meaning and provided a response model by which the adequacy of the reader's response can be judged. At times the interaction between questioner and reader predominates to such an extent that the reader attends mainly or even exclusively to the questions. Some comprehension questions and exercises lead the reader to focus minimal attention on the actual text. Any mediation of the teacher should be such that the reader will be encouraged to commune directly with the author. Comprehension in the terms of this goal might be more accurately gauged by viewing the child as the questioner rather than an answerer. That is, we might make better judgements about the child's ability to comprehend by encouraging the child himself to ask the questions. Such a response situation would be sufficiently unconstrained and open-ended to allow for proper evaluation of comprehension. Information to complement our perceptions of the reader's understanding could also be drawn from the judgements children make and the opinions they express about what they read.

It must be remembered that an individual's interpretation of a written utterance will seldom, if ever, concur precisely with the intent of the author. The reader will always infuse something of himself into the interpretation. This is a continuous activity that takes place throughout reading. It does not depend on a sudden flash of insight at the termination of a reading task.

Thus the assessment of comprehension should be primarily concerned with the way the child builds up patterns of meaning within a flow of language. Such a process would be better termed 'comprehending behaviour'. It is discernible when children set up expectancies during their reading, when they make predictions on the basis of the grammatical context and make guesses about the meaning of unfamiliar words.

Such behaviour is demonstrated when children make intelligent mistakes in their reading. Thus, in a group of children confronted with 'The three young boys were playing in the garage', most readers initially read this as '. . . in the garden'.

Others substitute 'your' for 'a' in the sentence 'What would you like for a birthday present?' It is clear that the children were not wedded to a single decoding strategy. They were anticipating as they read rather than tortuously processing the material visually. They were utilizing something other than the visual cue system.

Miscues, such as the examples above, may not be detected by the self-monitoring systems of efficient readers. The competent reader is most likely to correct a miscue only if the grammer is unacceptable or his response is not consistent with meaning in the surrounding context.

Efficient readers are able to engage in comprehending and self-correcting behaviour because they know that words must:

Make sense with other words with which they are used, (The eggs were sizzling in the frying p — n.);

Fit the other words grammatically in terms of function, (Small burrows in the s — nd are the homes of the rabbits.);

Fit the other words grammatically in terms of inflexion, (The man f — ll down the ladder.).

The efficient reader will be the one who can tell why words like 'pin', 'send' and 'fall' are inappropriate in the examples above.

The efficient reader is basically one who is 'tuned-in' to the language of the author.

He will correct misplaced inflexions in his oral reading. He will make repetitions to confirm the plausibility of his utterance or he will make regressions seeking further cues in the text to help him elucidate the meaning.

Such children will be able to 'fill the gap' in a text or

complete a phrase or operate with a line of print partly obscured. They are versatile in their utilization of a variety of cue systems to produce and check a response. They clearly demonstrate that they understand reading to be a search for meaning. In summary, evaluation of this objective should be concerned with discovering whether the child is primarily interested in what the author is saying rather than merely producing sounds for printed words.

The third major goal in the teaching of reading deals with decoding. This does not just mean the child's ability to match sounds with graphic symbols, an activity that is usually termed 'recoding'. Decoding means the interpreting of words as units of meaning not just units of sound. It is achieved in a context of language and experience and stems essentially from the child's ability to analyse words as language units. We could relate it to hypothetical stages which children pass through as they come to understand more about learning to read.

Thus, word attack skills and knowledge of the conventions of reading could come into existence as the following sequence of abilities is acquired:
— Speak and understand language, making discriminations between sentences and between words.
— Analyse phonemes within spoken words.
— Synthesize phonemes.
— Match graphemes with phonemes.
— Utilize the left-to-right principle of orthography.
— Analyse words into graphemes.
— Recognize printed words using various cues.

Beyond these abilities the efficient reader needs only to be able to:
a) Respond to the words signalled by print as if they were spoken words.
b) Decode printed words directly.

It is important to stress that evaluation in this area should not lead to the practice of teaching children to laboriously analyse words as they are met. Children going through the mechanical exercise of making responses to a series of visual stimuli can become so preoccupied with the act of responding that they fail to think. Because reading is thinking stimulated by print it should flow as spontaneously and naturally as the spoken language.

The efficient reader selects the minimum number of cues and, guided by his experience and knowledge of language, makes predictions which he confirms or rejects on the basis of semantic and syntactic acceptability.

Inefficient readers lumber themselves with the task of grappling with too many cues and this places inordinate demands on their memories. The evaluation of ability to decode therefore should be directed towards the reader's skill in selecting cues and categorizing them appropriately.

There is one vital decision teachers must make in regard to the evaluation of reading skills. Is the lack of skills always to be seen as the cause of reading failure or is failure in reading the reason why skills fail to develop? Skills in reading grow out of success in the task. They are acquired naturally when the child perceives that his existing strategies are inadequate and is motivated to seek new ones. Teachers involved in evaluation might differentiate between those children who need skills and those who have been taught the skills but do not apply them. Regrettably, many children learn and master skills in ignorance of their relevance to reading.

Many theorists have tried to list the skills that constitute reading ability. But reading does not depend on mastery of the sum total of these separate skills. It depends on the integration of a variety of components (linguistic, perceptual, cognitive, mnemonic, experiential) in a scheme of cognitive operations and applied to a reading task.

Evaluation in Practical Terms

The most profitable evaluation will occur when the teacher herself devises the evaluation procedures, basing them on her knowledge of the reading process, the resources available and her understanding of her pupils. Some type of diagnostic survey may be the best means of assessing skills, strategies and reading habits. It will be necessary for the teacher to arrange such items in accordance with the priorities she has established for the reading programme. She may group the items in terms of attitudes, knowledge and skills. She may classify them as either long term objectives or as short-term ones where the problem can be narrowed down to single teachable items. Such systemization in a survey will facilitate the grouping of children according to their needs. It may reveal that emphasis should be put on the broad reading environment. Or it may indicate that it should be put on achieving immediate and tangible goals.

Much of the information for a diagnostic survey can be gleaned by observing the child, by talking to him, by having him read passages (perhaps graded in difficulty) and covering a variety of topics and prose styles. A one-to-one pupil/teacher conference will usually be necessary to identify signals that indicate progress or difficulty. Depth of reading will be reflected in the way the child handles open-ended tasks related to the passages. The sensitive observer will note emotional reaction and creative or critical response. She will observe how well the reader adapts to the various purposes that exist for reading (e.g. reading for amusement, skimming for an overview, scanning a list, reading a poem, proof reading, oral reading to an audience, study activities, etc.). She will record the pupil's reading interests.

The following is a sample of questions the teacher might include in a diagnostic survey:

— Does the child have the language used in talking about reading? Does he know what letters, words and sentences are?
— Can he verbalize his thoughts on how he learns or how he can't learn to read?
— Are factors of attention and concentration involved?
— Is there open dislike, boredom or lethargy?
— Does emotional distress accompany a reading task indicating psychological discomfort or frustration?
— Do the words he is trying to read actually exist in his own language?
— How effectively does he utilize library resources?
— How wisely does he choose reading matter?
— What does he expect to gain from reading?
— How well has he acquired self-correcting strategies?
— Can he vary his reading rate?
— Is he sensitive to the various punctuation marks?
— Does he know what is indicated by the various printing devices like italics, boldface type, etc?
— Does he refuse to attempt unknown words?
— What is his preferred strategy in attempting unfamiliar words?
— Does he understand that the correct pronunciation of some

words can only be determined by reference to a dictionary or by asking someone who already knows?
— Does he know that correct pronunciation and meaning depend on the context e.g. 'desert', 'content'?
— Can he recognize familiar words in inflected form?
— Does he relate familiar words to phonemic and graphemic principles of the language?
— Can he focus on pronounceable combinations of letters without placing too much emphasis on individual letters?
— Can he make appropriate generalizations about orthographic shapes? (e.g. a *a* A are different shapes that signal the same letter whereas, c e a o are similar in shape but signal different letters).
— Can he describe how he works out the pronunciation of nonsense words? e.g.
    a) dalk, bine, rait (comparison to known word);
    b) compound words — bitrun, rinemiz, looptake
       little words in large — silbe, repine, robsip
       root word, prefix, suffix, inflectional ending — adwil, vonly, daling (structural analysis);
    c) bime, cler, swean (phonic analysis and phonic generalization).

Conclusion

Like his ability in speaking, listening and writing, a person's ability in reading is something that grows for as long as he learns. It will improve as vocabulary and language develop. It will be retarded by bad teaching or the lack of opportunity to become involved with reading. Its growth will be influenced by the pressures, self-generated or otherwise, leading the child towards efficiency in reading. But preoccupation with scoring, grading and keeping records can interfere with proper teaching and learning.

Evaluation in reading involves something other than administering one or a series of tests and compiling a set of numerical results for each child so that he can be compared with others in a group. Such activities may serve only administrative ends.

Reading by children should be seen primarily as an experience rather than an exercise.

It would be desirable at the outset to try and create an environment where anxiety does not exist, where teachers and pupils cooperate to use diagnosis in a mutually satisfying way, and where the children can learn progressively to appraise their own achievement. If ability in reading is the key to academic success, there is need for the evaluation in the context of effective teaching to lead to the improvement of attitudes, understandings and abilities among all children.

A new approach to evaluation in reading is thus called for in which teachers fully define objectives and then consider the various facets of the reading process and finally the backgrounds, capabilities and aspirations of their pupils.

Tremendous advances in educational theory have left a serious gap between theory and educational practice. Schools must accept the responsibility to become acquainted with research findings and innovative educational techniques and then interpret and evaluate them in the classroom.[2]

Home or School? Which is More Important for Pupil Achievement?

Recent research in the USA (J.S. Coleman et al., *Equality of Educational Opportunity*, US Government Printing Office, 1966) is giving educators second thoughts about the belief that the home background of youngsters is more important to their academic achievement than anything the schools do.

This is perhaps the major impression that emerged from a conference of many of the world's educational authorities who met to ponder the implications of a study conducted by the International Association for the Evaluation of Educational Achievements. The study, surveyed 250 000 students and 50 000 teachers in twenty-two countries.

Because of its profound social and political implications, the issue of home v. school has stirred much controversy in the United States since 1966, when the Coleman Report suggested that wide discrepancies in academic performance were more closely related to variations in home background than to variations in school quality.

The inference many drew was that it was futile to pump

more money into schools until the cultural gap between the rich and poor had been reduced.

But the sociologist who started it all, Dr James S. Coleman of the University of Chicago, told the conference that the new results 'suggest to me somewhat more hopefulness about schooling than we had in the past.'

It is not that the association's finding's contradict the previous studies. Rather, they have added many ambiguous notions and pinpointed the difficulty in interpreting broad statistical studies that, however sophisticated in conception, are only crude measures of complex social phenomena. Increasingly, social scientists are coming to recognize the limitations of the mathematical techniques of analysis that they have been applying to social problems.

'What we call home background may be a cumulative effect of home and school that is very difficult to disentangle,' said Professor Alan C. Purves of the University of Illinois, one of the authors of the association's reports. 'A child is the product of all his past — his own, his parents', his teachers'. You simply cannot say it is either home or school.'

Perhaps the most intriguing result of the study was that while home background did seem to play an important role in reading, literature and civics, school conditions were generally more important when it came to science and foreign languages.

This was considered significant because the Coleman conclusions were based only on reading and arithmetic scores in the United States, and the suggestion that certain subjects might be more amenable to school influences was taken as an encouraging sign by many.

Why this should be so is not clear, but one theory is that reading is very closely related to language acquisition, which starts at home, while science and foreign languages are more school-oriented. Whatever the case, the results underscore the hazards of interpreting social science.

The association's study tested children in six subjects and then attempted to correlate their achievement with five hundred independent variables presumed to be indicators of home background and learning conditions — such as the number of books in the home, parents' occupation, type of school, class size, amount of homework and attitude.

Then, by subjecting the figures to a complex technique known as regression analysis, the study sought to trace the variations in performance to variations in background and in schools. This method, which is at the heart of the debate, tells nothing about the *effect* of the home on levels of achievement. It merely says that the wide variations in achievement among children are more closely related to variations in home background than to differences between schools. This is not to say that schools do little; one explanation is that schools are so homogeneous, at least in comparison with homes, that their effect is hard to measure.

Moreover, in a cross-sectional study such as IEA's, cause-and-effect relationships are only implied, not proved.

On the average, the study was able to account for 39% of the performance variance in all countries, according to Dr T. Neville Postlethwaite, former executive director of the Stockholm-based IEA. This means that 61% of the variance remains unchanged.

Many of the participants in the meeting, held at the Harvard Graduate School of Education, harboured the hope that much of this portion was traceable to school conditions that had escaped detection.

Home background was found to account for 11.5% of the variation on the average for all subjects in all countries, and learning conditions amounted to 10% on the average.

Behind the debate on methodology were some fundamental questions about the premise of such studies. These doubts were expressed most forcefully by Ron Edmonds of the Harvard Graduate School of Education, who charged that the study was encouraging 'pernicious' policies because it was based on 'political and theological parameters' that precluded basic questions about schooling for students of low economic status.

Rather than make students conform to the standards of researchers, he said: 'What is wanted is interaction in the life of the school so as to compel a more effective instructional response to those who profit least from prevailing arrangements.'

His complaint was never fully answered, and the conference went on to explore the myriad implications of the study — for curriculum, for allocation of resources, for government policymaking and planning.

A New Look at Initial Reading

'Present approaches to the intial teaching of reading . . . may focus mistakenly on the very features which characterize unsuccessful rather than successful reading.' Thus spoke Dr Margaret Clark at an important seminar in language and learning held in Scotland.[3]

One main trouble, she said, is that research has concentrated on children who have failed to learn to read, rather than on what happens to successful readers.

Drawing on a great deal of recent research, Dr Clark showed up the negative aspects of a lot of current practice, and suggested lines which might lead to a more positive approach. She questioned the value of 'reading readiness' tests: 'There is probably no single aspect of the reading readiness battery which is an absolute barrier to learning to read for all children under all conditions of tuition.' She raised doubts about 'auditory discrimination' tests, which may test general and linguistic competence as much as refined auditory discrimination, and tests which check vocabulary rather than syntax.

Too much emphasis may be placed on training skills, such as the precise visual scanning of letters or words. Knowing or predicting what is likely to come next is an important element in both reading and language use in general — and this anticipation is based on skills other than simple comprehension.

Reading materials have often concentrated on repeating and building vocabulary, and not on meaningful sentences — producing language that is not only stilted and 'un-English', but worse, 'unpredictable'.

The importance of syntax in early reading materials is now being appreciated as evidence is appearing that children in learning to read can make use of their implicit knowledge of grammar.

But it was not enough to introduce new approaches — based on language generated by the children and teacher — such as *Breakthrough to Literacy*. It would be interesting to investigate what happens when competent, experienced teachers with different philosophies use parts of *Breakthrough* materials.

The solution does not lie in more pre-packed programmes. A programme for one group of children will not transfer unmodified to another. But programmes aimed to broaden children's language uses, and their appropriateness in specific situations, could help not only children but teachers also to achieve 'a greater awareness of the needs and potential of their children'.

Dr Clark suggested that too much attention had been focused on the language and other shortcomings of children (and their families), and too little on the language and other shortcomings of teachers (and schools). She said that success may depend not only on the child's competence in language, but on the language of instruction used by the teacher, and she questioned the idea of language 'deprivation', when used, of children who were often bombarded with speech (including constant television) at home.

Dr Clark suggested several positive lines of research. Studying how children on the way to being successful readers talked as they were learning, their mistakes and self-correction; finding ways, not of correcting specific deficiencies, but by-passing them; looking at the preparedness of schools to suit their teaching both to the task and to the children, rather than at the readiness of the child.

Researchers might study the different mistakes made by children taught by different methods. They might consider the specific value of reading aloud — by teachers and parents — not just the motivational value.

Dr Clark suggests that parents may often be doing much more than motivating children. 'In language teaching . . . parents may have been compensating for the deficiencies of the school.' Parents' contribution should be measured in more sophisticated terms than numbers of visits to the school, or books in the home, or socio-economic class.

Finally, particular attention needs to be paid to whether learning reading involves a sequential progression through a hierarchy of subskills to higher order skills. 'It may be that some of these steps are merely hurdles — or barriers — interspersed as a result of the types of approach to the teaching of reading employed in the schools.'

In her book, *Young Fluent Readers* (Heinemann Educational, 1976) Dr Clark studies the characteristics of good, early readers and the implications these have for the teaching of reading.

Some Causes of Learning Difficulties

There Is No Reading Problem

There is no reading problem. There are problem teachers and problem schools. Most people who fail to learn how to read in our society are victims of a fiercely-competitive system of training that requires failure. If talking and walking were taught in most schools, we might end up with as many mutes and cripples as we now have non-readers. However, learning to read is no more difficult than learning to walk or talk. The skill can be acquired in a natural and informal manner and in a variety of settings ranging from school to home to the streets. The conditions for natural learning are minimal and certainly not mystical or technically complex. [4]

Pre-School Influences on Learning Ability

Research work carried out over the past eighteen years at the Centre for the Study of Human Development at the London University Institute of Education has confirmed the findings of other studies related to the socio-economic environment of early childhood.

By the time the child from a professional or semi-professional home reaches school age he already has, on average, an IQ score twenty-five points above that of a child from a home in which the father is an unskilled or semi-skilled worker.

Judged on verbal ability alone, marked differences showed themselves in girls by the age of eighteen months. Dr C.B. Hindley, the Director of the Centre, argues that both hereditary factors and early environmental influences bore on the child's ability to respond to school work. He also thinks that children who had enjoyed a culturally enriched infancy 'may have some of the effects more or less permanently embodied in the functional qualities of their nervous systems'.

Some of the factors found to influence intelligence and verbal ability included: the variety of toys, books and educational experiences provided by the parents; the parents' use of language and their encouragement of speech in the child; the emotional atmosphere in the home; the child's emotional adjustment; and the breadth of the mother's vocabulary.

Large differences observed in IQ and verbal ability between children from contrasting social classes do not diminish during the school years and the Centre urges steps to be taken which would increase the level of intellectual stimulation in early life for children in the lower socio-economic groups.

There is as strong a case for the general provision of pre-school education as there is for compulsory education after the age of five years, and for active efforts to educate parents in ways to help their children.

Reading and IQ

Within the normal school population (i.e. excluding children with IQs of 70 and under), there are likely to be as many children whose reading is above average for their age and intelligence as there are whose reading is below average — whatever that average is. This has emerged from a major study by a team from the Institute of Psychiatry at London University, which looked at five huge samples — each of at least 1000 — covering four age groups (from nine-year-olds to fourteen-year-olds) in both urban and rural settings.

The average for the group was used as a measure, because of the problem of deciding what the expected level of achievement should be. They found that this was closely related to mean IQ level, which also left as many children on either side of the watershed. One of the most interesting by-products of the study, in fact, was the finding that IQ and reading achievment do not always bear the same relationship to one another. Reading deteriorates far less steeply than IQ; it also improves far less steeply than IQ.

Learning Difficulties Can Have Their Origins Before Birth

Albert   Tansley,   Inspector   for   Special   Education, Birmingham, has been particularly concerned with the identification, assessment, and prescriptive education of young   children   in   ordinary   schools.   His   research, experimental work, and writings related to learning disabilities, both general and specific, have made a unique contribution to special education in many countries.

In a recent talk he claimed that a child born after a disturbed pregnancy was more likely to have learning difficulties than an average child, and that as many as 30% of British children were born with this 'at risk' condition.

'Early identification is the only way to cure children with learning disabilities,' Mr Tansley said. 'Basic remedial methods should be taught to all primary school teachers to enable them to assess and treat problem children.'

He strongly opposed any suggestion that children with reading and learning difficulties should be taught in special schools, and went on to say that:

Segregation is out but individualized education is a must. Teachers should be trained in class management and ways of recognizing the uniqueness of all students.

Training teachers to assess difficulties in children should be a top priority.

Teachers should not be instructed to use standard intelligence tests in their quest to detect disabilities in young children.

Rather than say that a child has an intelligence quotient of 43 and label him an imbecile, they should be trained to reason why he is backward.

Mr Tansley said that intensive in-service training courses for teachers in Birmingham had produced school staff capable of handling problem children. This had lessened the incidence of children with learning disabilities becoming delinquents in later life because they felt frustrated.

He said that while it was likely that many adult emotional problems resulted from learning difficulties in youth, it was also probable that many infant learning disabilities were caused by early emotional stress.

Some Principles Underlying a Reading Programme

The most decisive factor influencing children's reading progress is the beliefs and attitudes of the staff about the *importance* of reading. In those schools where the staff consider reading of prime importance, and favour an early beginning

. . . children do learn to read, early and well, *almost regardless* of the media, methods or procedures adopted. [5]

Reading Readiness Criticized

A key idea long held by teachers has been refuted by two well-known researchers in the field of reading. Dr John Downing and D.V. Thackray, in *Reading Readiness* (Hodder and Stoughton, 1975, 2nd edn).

In a critical review of the evidence that children cannot learn to read before a certain age, the authors explode the concept of 'reading readiness' that has dominated much practice for the past thirty years. They conclude that:

> There can be no decisive answer to the question 'When is a child ready for reading?' because there is no single criterion that applies to all children or to all learning situations.

The teacher is the best judge of when to start. The authors offer a 'reading readiness inventory' to help teachers develop their observation and recording of a child's progress. It covers physiological factors such as vision, hearing and speech; environmental factors such as home experience; and intellectual skills such as whether a child understands the meaning of words or why we have a written language.

When we say a child is 'unready for reading' what we really mean is that *a gap exists between the child's present capabilities and the tasks we are asking him to undertake* in learning to read. The essential question now is 'how can we close this reading readiness gap?'

In their historical review of the concept of reading readiness, the authors query most of the old reasons why a child was said not to be ready.

These fall into three practical categories according to whether the teacher can do nothing; rather little; or a great deal about them.

1. Factors of No Importance

These are red herrings which distract teachers' attention from factors which they really can do something about:

a) *General physical maturity* (a favourite in woolly child-development lectures);
b) *Dyslexia* or *word blindness*. There is no scientific evidence for the allegations that these are important factors in reading readiness. On the other hand —
c) *Intelligence* is the best authenticated factor in reading readiness, but there is not much the infant school teacher can do about it.

2. Factors of Proven Significance, but Not Often Requiring the Teacher's Concern

These are:
a) *Vision, hearing and speech.* Most normal children come to school perfectly ready for reading as far as their eyes, ears and tongues are concerned. Speech deviations are more often a problem with otherwise normal children. The teacher's immediate role is referral to the qualified specialist.
b) *Emotions and personality.* The infant school teacher will rarely meet a child who is unable to begin reading because of a need for psychiatric treatment. More often, she may find signs of frustration or tension *after* reading has begun. This is a signal that the reading tasks are too difficult and must be made easier (the other side of the readiness gap).

3. Important Factors Frequently Occurring

In this category, we find:
a) *Sex differences.* There is a tendency for girls to get ahead in reading and this is probably due to the misconception which some boys have that reading is a feminine activity (e.g. mothers more often read bedtime stories, infant teachers are usually women, beginners' books are often more suitable for girls). The moral is: take special measures to ensure that boys find reading masculine.
b) *Home background.* Children from poorer home backgrounds often have difficulty in reading. This is no more an excuse for fatalism than the fact that a pupil happens to have been born a male. Activities need to be provided which will improve the child's attitudes towards, and

abilities in, linguistic and intellectual tasks. The same is true of children from minority immigrant groups; the school has to begin to compensate and provide for the different or inadequate experiences furnished by their home environments.

c) *Motivation.* Despite superficial appearances to the contrary (usually implanted by over-anxious parents), the evidence of research is quite clear — normal children come to school with little motivation to learn to read. Thus, most school beginners are motivationally unready. Indeed, it is no exaggeration to state that the single most important function of the infant school is to create and then nourish *intrinsic* motivation for reading. How? By sharing the truly valuable fruits of reading with children from the very beginning — i.e. finding out how to do interesting things from books, and discovering that books are a delightful source of entertainment.

d) *Perception.* Most normal children seem quite able to discriminate visually between small shapes such as alphabet letters. Their auditory discrimination, however, is usually much less well developed. Recent research in Britain as well as in America and the Soviet Union stresses the great importance of this ability to discriminate the sound units in words. This is a learned ability, and therefore the child's progress in developing auditory perception readiness depends on the teacher's provision of appropriate experiences. This definitely does not mean teaching either the names or the sounds of letters. Research shows that, for beginners, letter-name instruction is valueless and that conventional phonics is very inefficient. What do help children's auditory perception are activities which make the sounds of language interesting realities — i.e. activities which involve *listening* for the *sound* units in *spoken* language before the written language is emphasized.

e) *Concepts of language.* This is the most recent discovery. If we say, 'listen to the sound in this word', psychologically, it may sound to a young child something like 'listen to the *blank* in this *blank*'. Again, appropriate activities can be provided which will develop these linguistic concepts so

necessary for talking and thinking about the reading task
— i.e. activities which will lead the child to *understand* the
meaning of such linguistic terms.

Fitting the reading to the child has been attempted in
several dramatic ways during the past decade — i.e. the efforts
to simplify the traditional orthography (t.o.) of English: Caleb
Gattegno's *Words in Colour*; Kenneth Jones' *Colour Story
Reading*; Sir James Pitman's *i.t.a.* All make the nature of the
decoding process of reading an alphabetic language clearer
for the beginner. *i.t.a.* (but not the colour methods) has the
same effect additionally as regards the encoding process of
writing. Research shows clearly that many children who are
not ready to read t.o. are ready to read *i.t.a.* — a clear
demonstration that the readiness gap can be closed by
changing the reading task.
Other aspects of the reading task can be changed to fit the
child's needs. The content of children's reading can be made
more appropriate for their backgrounds. Working-class
children can read about familiar situations. Even if the publishers don't produce enough (or any) such books, teachers can
make 'home-made' ones with their pupils.

Children can read any word they speak. One of the greatest hoaxes in
all of educational pedagogy is that which says that reading
vocabulary must be developed in a predetermined logical sequence.
It just isn't so. Linguists tell us that when a child comes to school he
has all the language equipment he needs in order to learn reading
and all the other skills of language. The trouble is that we don't use
his equipment. We contrive artificial systems of language
development and methods of teaching reading, and we impose them
on children. It is almost as though the child has to learn two
languages in order to be able to read — one for communication and
one to 'get through' his reading books. [6]

Look-and-say, or the whole word method, plays little if any part as
an aid to learning to read as such, because it does not help a child to
decode unfamiliar words unaided. It does, however, provide an
invaluable introductory stage in which the child is prepared for the
task of learning to read: he learns to recognize a few familiar words,
although he cannot make fine distinctions between words of similar
graphemic pattern; he gains some knowledge of the sense of purpose
in print; he learns to operate in a left-to-right sequence if two or

more words are strung together; he begins to develop a notion of correspondence, albeit a hazy one, between sound and symbol; and he can achieve a form of 'reading' which, although it merely means that he can loosely recognize a few familiar words, does have deep motivational significance, in so much as a child who thinks he can accomplish a task is more likely to do so with greater ease than one who does not. If this distinction, between the preparatory function of look-and-say and learning to read itself, is maintained, it is possible to gain a clearer appreciation of the exact process of learning to read.[7]

On the evidence now available, it is impossible to determine which of the current methods of teaching reading is the best. Each has advantages and limitations and no method produces the same results in all situations. The latter finding suggests that other factors affect progress in learning to read. Different methods emphasize different aspects of reading and start pupils on different roads to maturity in reading. To become an efficient reader one must sooner or later acquire maturity in all the essential aspects of reading. As a rule the best results are obtained by stressing both meaning and word recognition from the beginning. However, many procedures have to be adapted to the culture, the language, and conditions and needs peculiar to each area. A sound reading programme for a given community can best be planned by those who have a clear understanding of both the basic principles that apply everywhere and local conditions and needs.[8]

Reading: Teachers, Methods and Attitudes

Over the past decade there has been a great deal of research into ways of improving reading. Teaching materials and methods have been examined and improved. New materials and sequential schemes have been developed. In the United States and Canada funds have been poured into research projects, studies, programmes and projects designed to discover ways of improving reading at all levels.

What is the main result of this research?

The tremendous range among classrooms within *any* method points out the importance of elements in the learning situation over and above the methods employed. *To improve reading instruction, it is necessary to train better teachers of reading, rather than expect a panacea in the form of materials.*[9]

A more recent American study concluded:

The results have indicated that *the teacher is far more important than the method.* Costly procedures such as smaller classes and provision of auxiliary personnel may continue to give disappointing results if teaching skills are not improved.

In other words, to improve children's reading attainment we should look first at the teacher and his training.

Methods are ways of thinking about a process. It is the teacher who interprets methods and puts them into practice so, consequently, contemporary research is concentrating more and more upon the qualities and procedures of 'the good reading teacher'. Researchers have tried to draw up a list of teaching tasks in order to assess a teacher's understanding and application of skills in such areas as selecting appropriate reading materials, grouping children, and judging improvement. Southgate and Roberts, in *Reading — Which Approach?* (Hodder and Stoughton, 1970) have examined teachers' choice of materials, medium, procedure, etc. in the light of basic, philosophical differences in approach to teaching reading.

There is evidence from research studies that the head teacher plays an important role in helping teachers to keep their interest and their enthusiasm for the teaching of reading (and, indeed, everything else).

One characteristic of influential heads appears to be their resourcefulness in involving teachers in decision-making. These heads encourage teachers to try out new or modified techniques and also seem to be able to get their teachers to evaluate what they are doing, so that they are continually re-examining their ideas.

The crucial factor, however, is the attitude of teachers. There is accumulating evidence regarding the relationship between teacher expectation and reading performance. Awareness of these research findings may not change an individual teacher's behaviour immediately, but it should be the first step towards such change.

Sex Bias in Reading

Reading schemes used in primary schools show rigid divisions between masculine and feminine behaviour which are foreign to most children. Research undertaken by Glenys Lobban, an English remedial teacher, confirms other research findings.[10]

She argues that if race and class bias in reading schemes are unacceptable, sex bias should be too. She examined the sex role content of six popular reading schemes: *Janet and John, Happy Venture, Ready to Read, Ladybird, Nippers* and *Breakthrough to Literacy;* 179 stories were coded.

There were only thirty-five heroines, but seventy-one heroes who, unlike the heroines, were frequently brave and adventurous. Boys took the lead and let the girls watch. Boys' activities were always more exciting, non-domestic and active.

The female world was almost entirely oriented towards domestic activity and child care. Only *Nippers* showed working mothers, and they were in a minority, whereas in reality many women have paid jobs outside the home. The only girls' physical activities were skipping and hopping.

The male world shown did not allow for expressive or caring behaviour. Boys' toys suggested future careers and their world was outside the home. They were the ones who would have the jobs, would be responsible for things in the world, apart, that is, from child care and cooking.

Only *Nippers* showed female, single-parent families: there were no male ones. Dad never cooked anything beyond a cup of tea, although he watched television a lot while mum and daughter bustled around preparing meals. The fact that many families share cooking, driving and housework, never came through.

Glenys Lobban concluded:

The reading schemes showed a 'real' world peopled by women and girls who were almost solely involved with domestic activity and whom the adventurous and innovative males might occasionally allow into their world (the rest of human activity and achievement) in a helpmate capacity. The world they depicted was not only sexist, it was more sexist than present reality, and in many ways totally foreign to the majority of children, who do have working mums, and at least some experience of cross-sex activities.

Learning to Read

A research project designed to seek ways of identifying the facts that contribute to fluency in reading was conducted in 1975 by some of the staff at the Victorian Education Department's Curriculum and Research Branch, Australia.

The central task of the project was to investigate reading strategies, but the subjects (100 eight-year-old boys) were asked an incidental question that produced some interesting results.

The question was *'How did you first learn to read — who taught you to read?'*

Only fifty of the sample indicated that they learned to read at school. Nine answered that they didn't know. The remaining forty-one claimed that they learned to read from: mum (9), dad (11), parents (10), big sister (4), brother and sister (1), grandmother (3), nursery-school teacher (2) and himself (1).

Stereotyping in Primary School Texts

Three teachers have completed a study which analysed a ten per cent random sample from one selection guide to primary school reading materials.

Their study found that primary school reading materials, if they are taken literally, show children that *two-thirds* of humans are male — who are 'large, colourful characters with a store of knowledge and skills and a great capacity for fun and adventure'.

Of the 22 775 characters studied, women were invariably at home preparing meals or minding children. Ninety-seven per cent of home duties in the reading materials were done by female characters but only six per cent of doctors, nine per cent of tradespeople and fewer than two per cent of skilled workers were women. Female characters generally appeared as 'smaller and less significant'.[11]

Sir Alec Clegg on Reading

I attended a meeting of the IRA last year in New Orleans — that is, of the International Reading Association. There were some 17 000 of us there and we really got down to the whole reading business. We talked of phonemes and graphemes, we looked at reading schemes by the score, we studied the phonology, the morphology, the syntax and the germantics of them, we identified consonant digraphs and grapheme-phoneme correspondences.

We even learnt the ways of constructing poems in which every line states something that isn't true and we perused publications such as *Thrice to Thine and Thrice to Mine: Nine Ways to Individualize Macbeth and Anything Else.* We listened to lectures on the best way of 'Selling Reading to Driver Education Teachers or How to Get Your Foot on the Clutch' and we even had a go at 'Transcendental Meditation and Reading'.

There was a 42-page programme of all these exciting things but the *pièce de résistance* was in the 90 000 square foot hall, where there were 300 stalls each selling its own reading device. Here the commercial boys had moved in with a vengeance to get their shares of the federal moneys which had been released to improve the nation's reading.

Now I am sure that in that hall there was much that was good and wise and efficient and highly commendable. But the overwhelming impression on me was of immense educational gimmickry, vulgarity and futility, and I could only thank God that the infant teachers I know take the view that, whatever a child might grow to hate as a result of his school experience (and most of us grow to hate something), reading he must learn quietly to enjoy.

10 Reading Failure

Because the reading process is highly complex, investigations into the causes of reading disabilities very rarely indicate that reading failure can be attributed to a single factor. There is usually a whole range of most complex factors simultaneously connected with reading difficulties with varying degrees of relationship between them.

Great care must be exercised in reaching conclusions concerning the specific causes of reading disability. It is frequently possible to state that certain factors are connected with reading problems but it is not always possible to differentiate between cause and effect.

There are three broad areas that may, singly or in combination, be the reason for reading failure.

1. Intellectual Factors

In general, the correlation between success in reading and the intelligence quotient is fairly high. Poor intellectual capacity will inevitably retard the progress of reading ability.

2. Language-Related Factors

A child needs a good vocabulary and a competent use of language before he can learn to read. Consequently backwardness in language development may lead to reading failure.

Reading develops from speech and a functional language is essential before children can learn to read.

Children need to have their own vocabularies in order to express their own ideas clearly.

It is now generally accepted that children should have developed an ability for oral expression before they can be expected to read and understand the ideas of others.

3. Physical Factors

There appear to be two ways in which reading ability can be affected by physical defects.

There is evidence to suggest that there is a pronounced association between auditory high frequency weakness and retardation or distortion in the understanding and articulation of speech and gross retardation in reading skills and written expression.

Illness or physical defects can fatigue children quickly and hence affect reading abilities.

Remediation: The Fourth R?[1]

Barry Carozzi

Many writers in the field of remedial teaching accept a model or description of the steps involved which may be summarized as follows:

Screening for identification
|
Diagnosis
|
Profile of skills
|
Development of an
appropriate programme
|
Segregation of the
group

As a first step, it is necessary to identify those children who are displaying serious weakness in reading. The means may simply consist of the teacher's own judgement, or some kind of reading test may be used. The latter is a fairly general practice in secondary schools; often, the new intake of children is tested in order to identify those with severe problems.

The at-risk group having been identified, a more detailed analysis and diagnosis is usually recommended. This diagnosis is generally regarded as the central task of the remedial teacher, since upon this all else, theoretically, hinges. In most cases, the diagnosis is behavioural: the child's reading behaviour is examined in terms of such characteristics as his knowledge of phonics, directional attack upon words, ability to blend, syllabification skills, comprehension, and so on. Some writers also suggest the use of IQ and personality tests. In some approaches, such as those of Delacato[2] and Frostig[3], visual-perceptual-motor skills, seen as underlying reading behaviour, are tested.

Very often, however, the diagnosis is limited to the reading behaviour of the child, and little attention is paid to other potentially crucial factors; for example, parental attitudes, previous experience of reading, and so on.

On the basis of this diagnosis, a profile of skills is developed, pinpointing the child's strengths and weaknesses, and an 'appropriate' programme may then be developed. The notion of an appropriate programme generally involves the segregation of the group for specialized teaching. Even in the so-called non-graded primary school, with its setting or ability grouping of students, as in the old opportunity classes, and in withdrawal groups such as those set up in many post-primary schools, students are segregated with the purpose of providing an appropriate programme and specialized teaching.

Weaknesses

This general model is widely accepted in the literature, and is the basis of most attempts to cope with reading problems, both in primary and secondary schools. There are problems associated with this broad approach, however:

☐ The approach centres upon the child himself — his reading behaviour and stage of skill development — and pays insufficient attention to other relevant causes of reading failure. The behaviourist argument goes something like this: 'If a child doesn't know how to blend, I teach him how to blend; if he doesn't know his sound-letter relationships, I teach him those. To know about "underlying causes" (such as delayed perceptual development, cultural deprivation, or frequent absences from school during the early primary years) is of little immediate value — in that you can do little about such factors. You must work with the child where he is now, building upon what he knows.'

There is a strong case, however, for arguing that the general nature of the underlying causal factors involved may have important implications for the type of teaching programme adopted. With children from a culturally deprived background, a programme emphasizing talk, discussion, excursions, and so on, aimed at widening the child's language and general knowledge, may be relevant; where emotional disturbance is a major factor, the development of therapeutic activities in a social context which is supportive and encouraging may be more relevant.

It is clear, too, that the problem affects not only the child, but his parents and teachers as well. The importance of their attitudes to the child's continuing learning also calls into question the validity of an approach which treats the reading problem in isolation.

☐ The approach assumes an expertise in diagnostic testing and interpretation possessed by few teachers in our schools. The implication is that an analysis of the 'profile of skills' will indicate the sort of programme relevant to the child's needs. This further implies the existence of an articulated, theoretical, empirically-based account of the way in which reading develops, and can be developed. Such theory, however, does not exist; and writers in the field often recognize this by urging the remedial teacher to be eclectic and to experiment with different approaches.

These are serious weaknesses of the current remedial teaching model.

Language Codes

Since the early sixties, considerable attention has been paid to the influence of home background factors on the child's learning at school. The influence of the home may be considered under two major headings: parental education and aspirations; the quality of the home as a learning environment.

There is considerable evidence to suggest that these two

broad factors largely determine the language which the child brings to school, the breadth of his experience, and his motivation for school learning.

In the area of language, the English sociologist Bernstein[4] has explored the relationship between social class and language. He suggests that we can look at such differences in terms of 'linguistic codes'.

The 'restricted code' is essentially the language of face-to-face context. The *meaning* of what is said is closely tied to the context of the talk — both the physical context and the context of the relationship between the people talking. It is the code of language used by people who know each other well. The 'elaborated code' is the language of intellectual discussion and of instruction. It is the language of the schools. The elaborated code user seeks to make his meaning clearly explicit, and to do this he chooses his words and phrases more carefully.

Things said in the restricted code may be almost meaningless outside the context in which the speaking occurs. Things said in the elaborated code 'stand on their own'.

Bernstein argues that working-class children are less able to use an elaborated code than middle-class children.

The following examples illustrate clearly the distinction between 'context-bound' (restricted code) and 'context-free' (elaborated code) language. Children were asked to talk about a series of drawings showing some boys playing football. In the course of the game, a window is broken.

Example 1: Context-bound

They're playing football and he kicks it and it goes through there it breaks the window and they're looking at it and he comes out and shouts at them because they've broken it so they run away and then she looks out and tells them off.

Example 2: Context-free

Three boys are playing football and one boy kicks the ball and it goes through the window, the ball breaks the window and the boys are looking at it and a man comes out and shouts at them because they've broken the window so they run away and then a lady looks out her window and tells the boys off.

In the first example, the language is closely tied to the

context — without the pictures, it is almost unintelligible. 'They', 'he', and 'she' are used without any clear reference. The second example, on the other hand, is relatively context-free — you don't need the pictures in front of you in order to make sense of what is said. Bernstein traces these differences in children's language to differences in the way language is used in the home.

There are many aspects of the home environment which are potentially important in language development — the size of the family, the extent of contact between child and adult, the opportunities for talk, the parents' attitudes to language use — all may play some role.

The parents' expectations and aspirations for their children may also determine the motivation the child brings to school.

The quality of the home as a learning environment — that is, for learning related to the later school learning — may also be relevant. The value placed on books and reading in the home, the extent to which parents read for themselves, or read to their children, may influence the child's attitudes to reading when he comes to school. Many parents, because they are not very literate, or lack confidence in their own reading, do not read to their children. Such children may arrive at school with limited experience of fairytales, stories, and so on. It is not uncommon to find children in secondary schools who know few of the traditional legends, myths, or children's stories.

The breadth of the child's experience with reading as a human activity plays a determining role in the child's later interest and success in reading.

The breadth and variety of the child's general experience may also be important in determining his response to what the school offers. For example, in 1969 a survey conducted at an inner suburban high school indicated that many of the children had never been to the city only four miles away. Such gaps in experience may have far-reaching implications for the school's programme.

It should be recognized, however, that the notion of 'breadth and variety of the child's general experience' is a difficult one to pin down. Children, no matter what their social background, are 'experiencing' widely all the time. What is crucial is the extent to which the child's experiences outside the school are relevant to the school programme, or, rather, seen by teachers as being relevant.

School Pressures

There are factors, too, within the school which may play a role in generating and sustaining failure by children. In 1955, Rudolph Flesch wrote *Why Johnny Can't Read,* a book which caused a furore in America (and elsewhere) among educationists and parents. Flesch attacked the 'whole-word' method of initial reading teaching and argued that the whole-word or look-and-say method produced many poor readers; children reliant on the general visual impression, who had no way of tackling unfamiliar words. The method was, in effect, look-and-guess. Flesch called for a reversion to 'phonic methods' of teaching reading.

   Flesch may be attacked on three grounds:

- [ ] The whole-word method was not as generally used as Flesch argued. In many schools, other methods were in common use.
- [ ] Flesch implied that hard and fast distinctions could be made between phonic and whole-word methods. Jeanne Chall has pointed out, however, that 'pure' methods do not in fact exist. All approaches to teaching reading involve phonic, whole-word, and kinaesthetic components.
- [ ] In fact, most children learn to read regardless of the method used in teaching them. However, in her review of research into the teaching of reading, Chall concluded that children taught initially by a phonic method did tend to read slightly better than those taught by a whole-word method. The advantage, however, was only slight, and many of the studies yielded results contradictory to Chall's general conclusion.

   The notion of 'readiness' has met with considerable criticism in recent years, largely because of the difficulties in specifying in detail what constitutes readiness to read. Nevertheless, it could be that too early a start for many children is made upon the teaching of reading. There is considerable pressure upon infant-school teachers to 'get the children reading', firstly from their colleagues in the higher grades ('I expect the child to be able to read by the time he gets to me'), and also from parents. To some extent, too, because of the considerable status given to reading, the success of the teacher may be equated with getting the children reading.

Often, too, it seems to be assumed that all children should start learning to read at the same time. Such an early stress on learning to read, in a context where success in reading is highly valued, may in itself be a contributory factor in failure.

Strategies

Holt, in *How Children Fail,* argues that the total context of the school, its organization and ethos, the way it goes about its task, constitute the major factor in causing failure. He argues:

Children are afraid at school, and they are afraid because they are taught in an atmosphere where failure is defined as 'dishonorable' and 'humiliating' rather than as an obstacle which generates constructive questioning and learning. In such a system children become motivated by 'success' which is based upon adult, or more specifically teacher approval, rather than self-accomplishment. To attain this goal students employ strategies in a game of 'winning', a game which may rob them of their basic enthusiasm and curiosity.

Teachers will recognize many of the strategies. A child may withdraw from the situation, either through actual absenteeism, or through day-dreaming, or preoccupation with his own activities. Assiduous copying is another strategy. Many poor readers will meet the apparent demands of a teacher by copying pages of material for a project or assignment. They will have little or no understanding of what they have copied, but that is irrelevant — so long as it appears that they have completed the task. Some children will say, 'I'm dumb. I can't do it', as a means of avoiding situations in which failure is likely. 'I won't do it'; 'I could do it if I wanted to. It's just that I don't want to'; 'That's kid stuff. I'm not doing that' — all of these are strategies children may adopt in order to cope with feelings of inferiority and the fear of humiliation and further failure. Other children become aggressive, acting out their anxiety in disruptive, perhaps destructive behaviour. Some studies have drawn attention to the high incidence of reading difficulty among delinquents, suggesting that the sense of rejection and inferiority resulting from failure in reading (and in school work generally) was a contributing factor to the delinquency.

Finally, the willingness of the school to be satisfied with the appearance of learning rather than real learning, may be related to failure. This distinction between real and apparent learning is best made through the well-known example concerning the philosopher and educationist, John Dewey, who once asked a class, 'What would you find if you dug a hole very deep in the earth?' When there was no response he repeated the question; again there was silence. The teacher chided Dr Dewey, 'You're asking the wrong question'. Turning to the class she asked: 'What is the state of the centre of the earth?' The class replied in unison, 'Igneous fusion.'

Where real learning has ceased to be the first concern of the child and the teacher; where both are satisfied, provided that it *looks* as though the child is coping — then those children with difficulties will not seek or receive the help they need.

Some Findings

My purpose thus far has been to draw attention to external factors which may bear some relationship to the child's failure. There are, of course, many factors within the child himself, which might account for his failure to learn to read: severe mental retardation, gross neurological impairment, and severe emotional disturbance are obviously related to failure in learning to read. But if we accept that 'nearly all children *could* become literate' — a view held by many writers, Ronald Morris[5] and Herbert Kohl among them — the problem becomes one of creating the right context for this to be achieved.

The following hypothesis, which is offered as a possible explanation of much of the reading failure in schools, rests on three empirically established propositions:

☐ The ratio of illiteracy for boys and girls is 3:1 (according to Vernon, *Reading and Its Difficulties*, CUP). This is a general finding in England, USA, and Australia.

☐ Illiteracy is not democratically distributed, but is most common in lower working-class areas — children from the homes of semi-skilled and unskilled workers are far more likely to have difficulty in learning to read than the children of professional, clerical, and skilled workers.

☐ There is quite a deal of evidence (e.g. Joyce M. Morris,

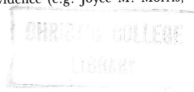

Standards and Progress in Reading, NFER, 1966) to indicate that if children are still non-readers by the time they are nine, the chance that they will ever read as well as their peers is relatively small (about 1:10).

What explanations can be offered for these three findings? There is some evidence to suggest that girls are more linguistically able than boys. These facts may be related to the sex-role expectations in the working-class home. Working-class boys are expected to be independent, assertive, active, and to identify with the father. Dependence upon the mother may be actively discouraged. The expectations for the girls, on the other hand, are quite different. Girls are expected to be 'mother's little helper', to be submissive rather than assertive, to identify with the mother.

Reading, in the school, is often an activity involving *dependence* upon the teacher; a *passive* activity — the children must sit and learn; and female-dominated. There are virtually no male infant teachers.

For the third empirical finding, there are at least three major possible explanations:

☐ There may be a critical stage, related to maturation and neurological development, in the child's life when optimum conditions exist for learning to read. If the child does not learn during this 'critical period', he may never learn to read adequately.

☐ The training of teachers other than those involved in infant teaching does not include much work on the teaching of reading. Thus, many middle-school primary teachers are not professionally competent to help the poor reader. A few may even assume that all the pupils can read.

☐ A third explanation has to do with the child's emerging self-concept and the teacher's expectations. After three years of failure, the child and his teachers come to see him as a non-learner, a failure. This then becomes a barrier to future learning.

A Hypothesis

On the basis of these general considerations, I would offer the following hypothesis. It is not intended to account for all reading failure. But it may help to account for a sizeable proportion of such failure.

Working-class children (especially the boys) come to the school from backgrounds which have ill-prepared them for the sort of demands the school will make. Their values, interests, aspirations, motivations, and language may well be at variance with what the school expects. They are 'unready' for reading; they may also be faced with the difficulty of relating to the 'non-language' of the Look-John-Look species of reader.

Because of pressures upon the teacher, the teaching of reading begins. The child fails initially, for any or all the reasons suggested above, and, as a result of this intitial failure, he is placed in the 'bottom group' for reading. Both he and his teacher come to see him as a 'bottom group' child; as a failure. He develops strategies which allow him to avoid the humiliation of public failure, but which are, in themselves, barriers to further real learning.

The traditional approach to teaching such children has been to offer instruction in the basic skills of reading in a special group. There is considerable evidence to support the contention that remedial teaching, as generally conceived, has been largely unsuccessful (see D. Moseley, *Special Provision for Reading*, NFER, 1975).

Finally, then, as possible solutions we might consider paying more attention to:

☐ Changing the general school context; this would involve making schools less competitive, and more supportive; it would involve abandoning ability grouping or streaming, much of the testing, and the preoccupation with marks; the development of individual children ought to be the focus, and in this comparison is totally unnecessary;

☐ Greater 'intellectual rigour' — that is, an emphasis on real rather than an acceptance of apparent learning;

☐ Introducing male teachers into the lower primary school classes;

☐ Taking the emphasis off reading in isolation from general language development, while creating a climate of interest in books and stories; then, the reading teaching must be organized in very small groups;

☐ Including more study of the teaching of reading in the training of all teachers, not just those preparing to teach in infant classes.

Appendix A:
A Language for Life

A Language for Life is the title of the report on the teaching of Reading and English published in February 1975 by the Committee of Inquiry, chaired by Lord Bullock.

The Committee listed 332 conclusions and recommendations, and seventeen principal recommendations, warning that it would be misleading to take these seventeen as a distillation of what they had to say.

We have been opposed from the outset to the idea that Reading and the use of English can be improved in any simple way. The solution does not lie in a few neat administrative strokes, nor in the adoption of one set of teaching methods to the exclusion of another. (Chapter 26)

The Principal Recommendations (Chapter 26) of the Report are:
- ☐ A broader, up-dated system for monitoring national standards.
- ☐ Positive steps to develop the language ability of children in the pre-school, nursery and infant years, including the involvement of parents, the improvement of staffing ratios in infant schools, and the employment of teachers' aides whose training has included a language element.
- ☐ A systematic language and reading policy in every school with a qualified teacher to help to implement it.
- ☐ Close consultation between schools, and the transmission of effective records to ensure continuity in the teaching of reading and the language development of every child.
- ☐ The promotion of support by appointing a network of advisers, extra staffing, increased budgets and closer links between schools and with parents.

☐ Screening procedures to prevent cumulative language and reading failure and to guarantee individual diagnosis and treatment.

☐ Additional help to pupils who are retarded in reading. Where they are withdrawn from classes for special help they should continue to receive support on their return.

☐ A reading clinic or remedial centre should be established in every educational region, giving access to a comprehensive diagnostic service and expert medical, psychological and teaching help.

☐ Special help should be provided for immigrants and illiterate adults.

☐ There should be a substantial course on language in education (including reading) for all teachers in training, whatever their subject or the age of children they will teach.

☐ An expansion of in-service education in reading and other aspects of English teaching is essential with courses at diploma and higher degree level.

Some significant quotes from the Report:

There is no one method, medium, approach, device or philosophy that holds the key to the process of learning to read. (6.1)

We would not be so unrealistic as to believe that every child should be a competent reader on leaving the infant school. But we would certainly be unhappy with a situation where the foundations of reading were not thoroughly laid there. (2.28)

We believe that the knowledge does exist to improve the teaching of reading, but that it does not lie in the triumphant discovery, or rediscovery, of a particular formula. (6.1)

We advocate, in short, planned intervention in the child's language development. (5.30)

There is no question of waiting for readiness to occur; with many children it does not come naturally and must be brought about by the teacher's positive measures. (7.11)

A priority need for *all* schools is a commitment to the speech needs of their pupils and a serious study of the role of oral language in learning. (10.30)

What has been shown is that the teaching of traditional analytic grammar does not appear to improve performance in writing. (11.19)

Primary and secondary schools often know little of one another's methods and aims. (14.12)

All genuine learning involves discovery, and it is as ridiculous, to suppose that teaching begins and ends with instruction as it is to suppose that 'learning by discovery' means leaving children to their own resources . . .; a child can learn by talking and writing as certainly as he can by listening and reading; to exploit the process of discovery through language in all its uses is the surest means of enabling a child to master his mother tongue. (4.10)

Learning to Read

The Report goes into a great deal of detail trying to define what is involved for a child learning to read. It comments that reading schemes have become increasingly colourful and well illustrated, but that too often there is little incentive to read the words rather than just look at the pictures. Schemes must also stand up to questions about parental roles, sex roles, attitudes to authority and so on as they are presented. (7.17)

The language in readers should, the Report claims, match the spoken language familiar to the child. If the syntax of the text does not match the syntax the reader expects, the ability to identify words will be slowed down. There are too many reading schemes whose language is stilted and unnatural. (7.18)

The survey of reading approaches conducted by the Committee showed that the great majority of teachers use a mixture of phonic and look-and-say methods. (25.18)

The major difference between teachers lies not in their allegiance to a method, but in the quality of their relationships with children, their degree of expert knowledge, and their sensitivity in matching what they do to each child's current learning needs. (7.20)

Before beginning any reading scheme children should know what the terms 'letter', 'sound' and 'word' mean. They should be able to discriminate between the shape and orientation of letters, know about left-to-right sequence, realize that letters are symbols that can represent sounds, recognize whole words as units of meaning not just symbols representing sounds; and respond to groups of words in terms of meaning not just as letters to be pronounced. (7.12)

Above all, children should have learnt to enjoy their encounters with words and sentences and with the meaning that lies behind them. (7.12)

If a child has had a satisfactory preparation before tackling a reading scheme we believe that the choice of scheme matters less than the teacher's knowledge of what a given scheme can and cannot do, and her ability to supplement it. (7.22)

The look-and-say scheme prompts three vital questions:
- ☐ How can a useful sight vocabulary be developed and enlarged?
- ☐ How are difficulties with phonic irregularity to be overcome?
- ☐ How can the child be helped to achieve independence in tackling unfamiliar words? (7.22)

When we come to phonic schemes there are questions of equal importance:
- ☐ How are children to be weaned from an early tendency to look for fairly simple relationships between letters and sounds?
- ☐ How can they be led to a greater dependence on context cues in handling unfamiliar words? (7.22)

The Committee would welcome the further development of the kind of scheme to which it is as difficult to apply such simplistic labels as 'phonic', 'look-and-say', 'linguistic' etc. as it is to attach such labels to the methods of competent teachers. (7.25)

Reading schemes should be ancillary to a school's reading programme and nothing more. Performance should provide teachers with diagnostic information, and there should be a great variety of supplementary materials for individual children who need practice or help of a particular kind.(7.25)

Several reading schemes at once can be used as part of the learning resources available, and the children's own writing should provide 'an ever-developing resource'. (7.25)

The most important factor for success in the teaching of reading is for teachers to be able to think clearly about sequence and structure in an appropriate reading curriculum for each individual child as well as for the class as a whole. Teachers must decide if a given objective is best achieved by individual work, work in small groups or class teaching. They must decide how much time to spend on reading, how to evaluate their teaching and monitor the progress of each child, and how to make the best use of other adults, including helpers, parents and older children. (7.30)

Every child should spend part of the day in reading or pre-reading activities. Teachers need to keep a meticulous check on progress, to make qualitative observations by listening to every child read several times a week, and ask questions to develop different kinds of comprehension. All children — not only under-achievers — need this attention. (7.31)
There is a place for class teaching as an effective and economic way of dealing with a specific skill. (7.31)

The value of the collective class experience needs to be reaffirmed, and it is exemplified at its best when all the children are sharing the enjoyment of teachers reading to them. (7.31)

In the middle and senior years of the primary school the Committee recommends that there should be three major emphases:

☐ Firstly, consolidating the early work and giving particular help to children who have failed to make progress.

☐ Secondly, maintaining and extending the idea of reading as an activity which brings great pleasure and is a personal resource of limitless value.

☐ Thirdly, developing pupils' reading from the general to the more specialized. (8.1)

Since reading is a major strategy for learning in virtually every aspect of education we believe it is the responsibility of every teacher to develop it. (8.9)

It is often difficult for many teachers to be fully aware of the complexity of reading and study skills that are second nature to them. (8.9)
Reading for learning should be made more effective, every pupil becoming 'an active interrogator of the text rather than a passive receiver of words.' These skills should be developed in close association with other language use, particularly talking. Group discussion based on co-operative reading is a valuable means of learning. Besides literal comprehension, children need to explore inferences in a wide range of materials — not only textbooks. (8.10)
The Report strongly emphasizes the importance of literature in the reading programme. Teachers must promote books, bringing the right book to the right child at the right

time, and getting groups of children to discuss their reading and explore one another's reactions to it. 'This is so much more productive and so much less forbidding than the obligatory written book review, where the pupil knows that his pleasure has inevitably to be followed by a chore.' (9.7 and 9.8)

Although there is a place for reading which relates to the child's own environment; fantasy, folk tales, and stories with unfamiliar settings and characters should be included in an effective reading programme. (9.10)

The main emphasis in teaching literature should be on extending the range of reading. 'True discernment can only come from a breadth of experience. Learning how to appreciate with enthusiasm is more important than learning how to reject.' (9.15)

Organization

It seems to us unfortunate that public debate has tended in recent years to oversimplify a complex situation and has often been conducted through a series of slogan-like headings. The conditions in which children learn most efficiently call for serious study, and in our view it seems naive to believe that a particular form of organization will itself guarantee them. (13.4)

The Committee comments on the debate about primary school organization. Advocates of the traditional pattern — basic skills in the mornings, and the afternoons for history, geography etc. — maintain that it ensures attention to correctness in writing and measured progress in reading which both parents and children like. Its critics say it limits the opportunities for learning, and all too often the practice of skills is unrelated to the children's other experiences.

We are bound to say that extreme attitudes on either side are unhelpful. Moreover they represent a situation that does not exist in schools in any such extreme form. (13.4)

The report reviews arguments for and against vertical grouping (grouping children of different ages in one class). Infant schools that pioneered such grouping had already introduced the integrated day, on the principle that subject barriers were artificial for young children. The chief criticism is that where children pursue their own interests, they lack direction and attention to basic skills.

So the survey looked at how schools using vertical grouping tackled the basic skills, compared with those that did not.

Seventy-eight per cent of non-vertically grouped classes with six-year-olds set aside time each day for attention to basic skills, compared with fifty-two per cent of vertically grouped classes. For nine-year-olds, the proportion of classes doing this was eighty per cent in both categories. (13.8)

There was no great difference between the two groups in their attention to phonics or the number of times they heard children read. There was almost exact correspondence in the time both spent on individual reading practice through graded schemes and other material (13.8 and 13.9)

With vertical grouping, 'the teacher must record with great care the progress and not merely the activities of each individual child.' Again the evidence showed few differences between different forms of organisation. (13.10)

School organization should depend on the needs of the children, the strengths and weaknesses of the teachers and quality of other resources, material and human. Organization should be capable of change: it is not good enough to adopt whatever is modish, or to cling to the best that could be managed in the past. (13.11)

Organization should reflect certain facts — 'all seemingly obvious but by no means always taken into account'. Children change as they grow older; children of the same age and social background differ widely in their attainment and interests, and the differences between them do not remain constant; children learn best what is useful to them. (13.13)

Our impression is that changes in organization within schools in recent years have not generally been matched by changes in class-room practice . . . We visited some classrooms using the 'integrated day' form of organization where the educational environment was less imaginative and demanding than that to be found in many 'traditional' classrooms. For example, when children moved to the 'language bay' they would take an assignment card and work to the instructions it gave . . . There was no interpenetration of language and the other learning experiences, and often little contact with the teacher. The system gave the appearance of allowing each child to work alone at his own pace. In fact, some of the work was as narrow in scope as the more 'formal' variety it has replaced, and it had the disadvantage of reducing the shared activity which gives opportunity for so much language. (13.12)

Organizational change needs careful thought and planning. It is no good changing and then still carrying on old practices. Nor should changes be introduced until the staff have had time to prepare for them. (13.12)

As children get older and more independent, most of them welcome access to teachers with more specialized knowledge. This development should be gradual — but change in organization usually comes, often with 'uncompromising abruptness', when children go to secondary school. The Committee do not believe there is an organizational solution for primary schools as distinct from secondary schools. Nor should organization remain virtually unchanged throughout the primary years. There should be gradual transition to a degree of specialism for older children and the report suggests ways of arranging this. (13.13)

Small-group and individual work is the best way to handle differences between children and the uneven development of individual children. Decisions to produce worksheets should take account of the importance of group talk for language development and for developing children's response to literature. (13.14)

Chances to work as a class should not be lost.

We talked to teachers who never read a story or a poem to the class, or talked to the children collectively. Indeed, some felt they would be wrong to teach the class or any part of it directly since this would compromise their commitment to a 'child-centred curriculum'. (13.14)

This represents a serious narrowing of opportunity. Some conventions of language, for example, need to be *taught* (not necessarily to a full class). (13.14)

Class organization should be flexible. Independent work by individuals and small groups is best and should be the principal form of class organization, with the class occasionally coming together to be taught or to work as a whole. Where such flexible organization is working success-fully, rigid timetabling is likely to interrupt learning. (13.15)

Reading Failure

There are many causes of reading failure; home and economic environment, sensory defects, limited mental ability, anxiety or depression. A limited number of children fail for no obvious emotional or extraneous reasons, and are usually called dyslexic. (18.5)

The Committee believes that the term 'dyslexic' serves little useful purpose other than to draw attention to a chronic and severe problem. It is not susceptible to precise operational definition; nor does it indicate any clearly defined course of treatment. Most of these children, however, do find difficulties with specific perceptual aspects of reading, and given skilled diagnosis and intensive help, most of them eventually learn to read. (18.5)

Certain factors are essential if success with remedial programmes is to be lasting:

☐ (i) A child's particular difficulties must be related to his whole linguistic development. The methods employed in remedial education are not intrinsically different from those employed in any successful teaching — the essence is that more time and resources go to adapting methods to individual needs and difficulties. (18.12)

☐ (ii) 'Fundamental is the teacher's ability to create warm and sympathetic individual relationships with the pupils, so that they are encouraged to learn through the stimulus of success .... Remedial work is not work for the inexperienced or indifferent teacher, but for the one who combines a high level of teaching skill with an under-standing of the children's emotional and developmental needs.' (18.12)

☐ (iii) Remedial help should be closely related to the rest of the child's learning wherever possible. Remedial work should not result in fewer opportunities for children to achieve success in other activities, such as crafts, drama and music. (18.12)

☐ (iv) There should be every attempt to involve parents, and help them to understand their children's difficulties. (18.12)

Most children who need help should be given this in their own schools — pupils who make progress in remedial groups should return to groups with their peers as soon as possible. (18.18)

The Committee is clear that language skills — from infants' talk to students' analysis — can and should be taught. They are highly critical of teachers in both primary and secondary schools who 'so misunderstand modern methods as to believe that they should never directly teach the children.' (Chapter 10)

However, they are no less critical of those who believe that skills can be taught by kits or exercises in isolation from pupils' other work. There is no evidence, they say, that grammar, spelling and punctuation exercises improve writing, unless they are taught at a time when they fit individual pupil's needs. (Chapter 11)

The Bullock Report *A Language for Life* (HMSO, 1975) is the most significant educational report since Plowden, and all teachers will find interesting, stimulating and practical suggestions in it.

Appendix B:
Reading Materials

It is indeed difficult to see how anyone learning to read can avoid the code. But can we not take the view that a child new to reading should use what he has already discovered about language — the meaning of what he hears, his interest in sounds and words, his facility with talking, as well as his newly-learned audio-visual skills — to help him master the code? And is not the purpose of breaking the code to get the message?[1]

Due to pressure of space it is not possible to describe all the reading materials currently available, so we have selected a variety:
- basic reading schemes for teaching reading
- reading series for consolidation
- reading materials as part of a total language programme
- books for enrichment.

The following publications contain evaluations of reading materials:
Brenda Thompson, *Learning to Read* (Sidgwick and Jackson, 1970).
George Pappas, *Reading in the Primary School* (Macmillan, 1962).
Vera Southgate and Geoffrey Roberts, *Reading — Which Approach?* (Hodder and Stoughton, 1970).
Vera Southgate, *Beginning Reading* (Hodder and Stoughton, 1972).
Alice Yardley, *Exploration and Language* (Evans, 1970).

Time for Reading (Ginn)
A sequential reading scheme for junior primary levels, based on:
- children's activities and interests;
- natural language patterns.

Materials include: basic readers, consolidation readers, pre-reading picture book and workbook, teacher's book of stories and poems, workbooks, wall pictures, flashcards (words and sentences), indicator cards, classroom labels, outline picture pads. The teacher's guide is very comprehensive.

Features:

— the continuous story element of the first reading book: the vocabulary is controlled but not obviously restricted and repetitive;
— artistic presentation and literary quality throughout;
— a child-centred programme.

Scott Foresman Reading Unlimited (Reading Systems Revised) (Scott Foresman)

A reading scheme based on natural language structures and children's interest. Levels 1-12, Junior Primary; levels 13-21, Senior Primary.

Materials include: for the teacher — teacher's read-aloud library, record books and cards, stencil master, magnetic boards and equipment; for the children — readers, pre-reading books, study books and practice pads, 'take home' books. A teacher's guide is provided for each reading level.

Vocabulary increase is steeper than that found in many basic reading schemes, but there is ample opportunity for consolidation.

Features:

— teacher's read-aloud library: at each level there are books of poetry and stories. This scheme recognizes and provides for the need for enjoyment and enrichment through literature of high quality while children are mastering the skills of reading;
— the development of comprehension skills in relation to both fiction and non-fiction material is an important part of the programme;
— literary quality and a variety of interesting art work and graphics are outstanding features of this scheme.

Beginning readers should be able to read short sentences with familiar words as wholes, and not as disjointed collections of words. It is important for students to understand that sentences have rhythm and that words in the context of a sentence are modified by each other. The written word should be referred to the rhythm and movement of the spoken word in the student's mind. The sentences in Dick and Jane readers are flat because no one would ever say them — they are manufactured to appear in basal readers and have no relationship to spoken language.[2]

Sparks (Blackie)

This reading scheme, for junior primary levels, has been devised for children in an urban environment, a world of flats, backyards, traffic, and playing in the park.

The stories are real and lively, and not burdened with a great deal of repetition.

Materials include: basic readers, consolidation readers, prereader, teachers' story book, teachers' manual, sentence and word matching cards.

Features:

— children living in inner suburban flats are likely to relate to these books about the Sparks family — father, a lorry driver; mother, works part-time at the supermarket; four children — living in Flat 77 at the top of a high rise development;
— at last there is a scheme which recognizes that some mothers work outside the home. (With so many married women in the workforce, there must be many children who do not relate to the family situations in most basic reading schemes.)

Reading 360 (Ginn) and *Magic Circle Books* (Ginn)

This sequential reading scheme is based on the latest research findings on linguistics, learning theory and the language experience approach.

Materials include: basic readers, stimulus pictures, activity cards, decoding charts, duplicating masters and teachers' manual. The *Magic Circle Books* are an extension library to the basic reading scheme.

The programme achieves a marked increase in vocabulary acquisition. The child reads highly meaningful materials from the beginning.

Features:

— there is a strong linguistic influence in the decoding process at the early levels of *Reading 360;*
— the *Magic Circle Books* contain a wide variety of material

— traditional fiction, modern fantasy and humour, poetry and non-fiction;
— literary style and illustrations are of high quality.

The Value of Writing

In writing, the child must construct his own words, letter by letter. The attention of eye and brain is directed to the elements of letters, to letter sequences and to spatial concepts. The child who writes a simple story is caught up in a process of synthesizing words and sentences. This building-up process is an excellent complement to the visual analysis of the text in his reading book, which is a breaking-down process. By these two processes the child comes to understand the hierarchical relationships of letters, words and utterances. He also confirms that the left-to-right constraint is applied to lines of print, to words within lines, and to letters within words. Although his knowledge of written language is severely limited, his early learning is patterned in a useful way and is not just scrambled.[3]

Breakthrough to Literacy (Longman)

Breakthrough to Literacy is a set of materials, planned on the following principles:
— literacy is best learned by the integration of writing and reading;
— reading should be closely linked with children's own spoken language.
Materials include: for the teacher — demonstration size sentence maker, magnetic teaching materials, teachers' manual, poetry book; for the children — sentence makers, word makers, readers on several levels, alphabet book, nursery rhyme cards and record.

Reading begins from the children's individual sentences which they make (with the teachers' help), using the 'core vocabulary' in the sentence makers. These are written into their own exercise books, and become their first reading matter. (Blank cards for 'personal' vocabulary are provided.)

The study of words is aided by the use of word makers — letters and letter combinations.
Features:
— the *Breakthrough* readers are derived from actual stories told by children in the literacy experiment that produced

Breakthrough to Literacy, and are highly meaningful to children. Illustrations are excellent;
— the provision of materials helps the teacher wanting to use a language-experience approach. However, organization for storage and handling of the equipment must be well planned, and children should be trained in independent use and care of it.

Language in Action (Macmillan Language Project)

These materials are concerned with reading in association with listening, speaking and writing. The scheme is designed to equip children with word attack skills.

Materials include: pre-literacy books, alphabet books and reading books, discussion pictures, duplicating masters, wall frieze, and teacher's resource book and supplements.
Features:
— the 'initial letter' books use tactile means to assist retention;
— stories are imaginative, funny and interesting;
— the importance of auditory discrimination at the pre-reading and initial reading levels is recognized;
— there is variety and quality in story, illustration and format.

Little Nippers and *Nippers* (Macmillan)

These readers are based on realistic environmental themes — the everyday experiences, joys, fears and griefs of children. They are appealing to all children, and especially to those who come late to books from a background devoid of reading materials.

The stories have excitement, adventure, suspense, fantasy and humour. The bright illustrations are closely allied to the text and reinforce the mood.

The texts echo the natural rhythmic speech patterns of children and adults.
Features:
— the *Little Nippers* achieve vocabulary control without the stilted dullness and meaninglessness of many first readers. Texts are simple, sentences are short, illustrations are lively and humorous, and content is meaningful and often amusing;

— an understanding of relationships, between members of the family, between adults, and between children, is an outstanding ingredient in the series. Dialogue is lively and realistic, and sometimes terse and insulting, as it is in everyday life;

— this series is one of the few that includes mothers working outside their homes.

. . . children's reading should derive more from what they themselves *actually* say (as distinct from when they are talking 'correctly') and from what their *real interests* are, than they often do in many reading schemes.[4]

Link-up (Holmes McDougall)

Link-up reading and writing activities are set in the context of today's children, especially the urban child or working-class parents. It gives special help to disadvantaged children.

Materials include: basic books, trailer books, build-up books, set of pictures, draw-and-write cards, lotto game, limpet cards (with self-stick words), and teachers' manual.
Features:

— printed signs and notices from the environment are used in the readiness stage to help children think about written language;

— the reading programme uses sentence structures based on children's natural speech;

— spelling patterns have been integrated from the beginning so that the teacher is able to begin phonic teaching in relation to children's reading;

— *Link-up* makes positive links with other classroom activities such as art/craft, science and mathematics.

The Beginning Beginner and *Beginner Books* (Collins)

This series of books for early reading is not a sequential reading scheme.

Although the books have very limited and simple vocabularies, short sentences and a great deal of repetition, the rhyming, word rhythms and humour save them from being dull.

Some books assist with phonics in an imaginative way using nonsense words.

Illustrations are bright and give clues to the reading matter.

Early I Can Read and *I Can Read Series* (World's Work)
This series is patterned along the lines of those described above.

An outstanding feature is the illustrations, e.g. the *Little Bear* books by Else Minarik, which are the backbone of the series. Maurice Sendak's illustrations are tender, humorous and beautifully designed.

Dick Bruna Books (Methuen)
This series can be classified as literature, rather than 'readers'.

Mild excitement and suspense in the story line, large print, simple and bright illustrations are features of the books.

Enrichment

Children should have access to beautiful picture-story books as well as readers at every level. Books by outstanding artists and writers are available now in paperback (e.g. *Picture Puffin* and *Faber Picture-Story Books*).

Children can be introduced to excellent literature at an early age. There are many books (for a range of ages) written by well-known authors who have given special attention to vocabulary control and suitability of content, meanwhile maintaining literary quality in style, presentation of themes and characterization, e.g.

Gazelle, Antelope, Reindeer (Hamish Hamilton).

Picture Puffin, Young Puffin, Puffin, Peacock (Penguin).

Faber Picture-Story Books, Faber Paperbacks (Faber and Faber).

The Acorn Library (The Bodley Head).

Early Bird Series (Kaye and Ward).

Pied Piper (Methuen).

It is extraordinary that in advertising pamphlets some publishers are suggesting that series of books for older reluctant readers (aged 12-16, reading age up to eight) are suitable for fluent readers of eight or nine years. The content of books for reluctant readers has been specially planned so that it is suitable for young adolescents. When there are superb series such as those above to delight fluent readers throughout the primary school there is no need for teachers to accept such alternatives.

Children who are at the stage of initial literacy should not be faced with 'readers' which are designed to practise word recognition. But rather they should be presented with books which describe life experiences which are relevant to them, in a way that adult books communicate about significant life experiences. In other words, if the first books children read are not works of literature, we are selling them short. For reading is not an end in itself, it is a means to experience. [5]

Appendix C: A Current Guide to Reading Materials

Publisher	Addison-Wesley Ltd, West End House, 11 Hills Place, London, W1R 2LR		Reading age
Reading materials	*Publisher*	*Brief description*	
Early Reading Programme (Penny Platt) Big Boy Friends For Big Boy Meet Some New Friends Do Some New Things	Addison-Wesley	Supplementary reading programme based on children's art. Combines language-experience approach with word attack skills. Full colour.	5-8 years
Badger Books (Patty Wolcott) The Cake Story The Forest Fire Where Did That Naughty Little Hamster Go? The Marvellous Mud Washing Machine I'm Going to New York to Visit the Queen (More titles available)	Addison-Wesley	Supplementary programme — 5 little books containing only ten different words in each. Rhythmic arrangement of words makes for easy reading. Full colour.	Pre-school

Workjobs (M. Lorton)	Addison-Wesley	101 manipulative activities for pre-reading and early reading.	Teacher reference
The Checkered Flag Series (Bamman) Eight titles Audio-visual materials also available for each text.	Addison-Wesley	High-interest, controlled vocabulary readers. Title deals with a different type of vehicle in a competitive situation. Hardback.	*Interest:* 11-15 years *Reading:* 7-10 years
The Time Machine Series (Darby) Eight titles	Addison-Wesley	Adventures in time and history. High interest supplement to basic reader at primary levels. Hardback.	*Interest:* 5-10 years *Reading:* 5-8 years
The Jim Forest Readers (Rambeau) Twelve titles	Addison-Wesley	High interest, low vocabulary series. Adventure-filled plots in the great outdoors. Hardback.	*Interest:* 6-13 years *Reading:* 6-8 years
Wildlife Adventure Series (Briscoe) Eight titles	Addison-Wesley	Appealing stories about man and his relationship with animals. May be correlated with natural sciences. High interest, controlled vocabulary. Hardback.	*Interest:* 8-12 years *reading:* 7-10 years
Happenings (Sullivan)	Addison-Wesley	Designed for reluctant readers in urban junior and middle schools. Characters are minority group teenagers. The books present realistic urban problems in contemporary settings e.g. a rock concert, a hippie pad. Controlled vocabulary. Hardback.	*Interest:* 13-18 years *Reading:* 9-11 years

	Publisher		Reading age
	Ward Lock Educational Co. Ltd, 116 Baker Street, London W1M 2BB		

Reading materials	Publisher	Brief description	Reading age
Take Part Books	Ward Lock Educational	Popular plays structured for participation by children with different reading ages. The Treasure Seekers Beaverbird Brer Rabbit Chitty-Chitty-Bang-Bang Parsley and the Herbs Flat Stanley Robin Hood Six Folk Tales Wizard of Oz Wind in the Willows Teachers' Guidelines	6-9+ years
Reading Workshops 6-10 and 9-13	Ward Lock Educational	Structured approach to development of reading skills.	6-10 9-13
Remedial Reading Workshop		Designed for interest levels 10 to 14.	6.8-9.1 years
Pre-reading Workshops 1 and 2		Multisensory kit designed to develop the necessary reading attitudes and skills which are tested by matching and sorting activities.	4-5 years

Publisher			
	Scott Foresman & Co., 1900 East Lake Avenue Glenview, Illinois 60025, USA		
New Open Highways	Scott Foresman	Reading programme for those reading below their chronological level. Phonetic emphasis.	5-12 years
Language & How to Use It	Scott Foresman	Pupils' & Teachers' books, 1-8. Child-centred language programme.	5-12 years
Reading Unlimited (Reading Systems Revised)	Scott Foresman	Comprehensive multi-level reading programme based on the Goodman theories that reading is a 'search for meaning'.	5-14 years
Publisher			
	Cassell and Co. Ltd, 35 Red Lion Square, London, WC1R 4SG		
Solo Books 32 titles	Cassell	Thirty-two graded readers encompassing many different literary styles.	8-11 years

Reading materials	Publisher	Brief description	Reading age
Publisher	Heinemann Educational Books Ltd, 22 Bedford Square, London, WC1B 3HH		
Reading: the Patterning of Complex Behaviour (Marie Clay)	HEB	Reference work related to the teaching of reading.	Teacher reference
The Early Detection of Reading Difficulties: Diagnostic Survey (Marie Clay)	HEB	Concepts about print test related to above. Test booklet also available.	Teacher reference
What did I Write? (Marie Clay)	HEB	Related to children's approach to print.	Teacher reference
Alpha to Omega (Hornsby and Shear)	HEB	The A-Z of teaching reading, writing and spelling. Accompanied by a set of flash cards.	Teachers reference

Read, Write and Spell (Leech and Nettle)	HEB	A systematically structured, four-stage programme of workbooks and flashcards.	Beginner level to reading age 10
The First Reading and Writing Scheme (Margaret Hooton)	HEB	A methodical, phonic approach to the initial teaching of reading; consists of teachers' book, practice book, dictionary and 4 wallcharts.	Beginner level
Stories for Today	HEB	Remedial Readers — interest age — 10-13 years.	6-7 years
Instant Reading	HEB	Remedial Readers — interest age — 9-12 years.	7½-9 years
Booster Books	HEB	Remedial Readers — interest age — 10-13 years.	8-10 years
Joan Tate Books	HEB	Remedial Readers — interest age — 10-14 years.	9-10 years
Wide Horizon Reading Scheme (Ridout and Serraillier)	HEB	Remedial Readers — interest age — 9-12+years.	7½-9 years
Heinemann Guided Readers	HEB	Remedial Readers — from Beginner Level to Upper Level — interest age — 11 years-adult.	
Winners (Kathleen Berman)	HEB	Remedial/Adult Literacy Readers — interest age — 12 years-adult.	5-11 years
Publisher	Holmes McDougall, Allander House, 137-141 Leith Walk, Edinburgh, EH6 8NS		

Reading materials	Publisher	Brief description	Reading age
Link-Up	Holmes McDougall	A basic reading programme that connects the printed word with children's speech, with their activities and interests, with their writing and their environment. Can be used with various approaches to the teaching of reading. Graded readers — Trailer Books. Link-Up Books. Build-Up Books. Teachers' Manual. Large pictures. Lotto boards and cards. 'Draw and write' word cards. Limpet words and cards.	Pre-reading to 8 years
Publisher	Longman Group Ltd, Longman House, Burnt Mill, Harlow, Essex, CM20 2JE		
Breakthrough to Literacy	Longman, (for the Schools Council)	64 Breakthrough books, Sentence Maker, Word Maker.	Pre-reading to 8 years.

	Publisher		
Longman Structural Readers	Longman	A series of graded supplementary readers in six stages.	6-12 years
Monster Books	Longman	12 graded readers in four sets.	$6\frac{1}{2}$-$7\frac{1}{2}$ years.
Bangers and Mash	Longman	14 graded humorous phonic readers using two chimps as main characters. Interest extends up to top primary remedial pupils.	5-$6\frac{1}{2}$ years
Olga da Polga	Longman	8 carefully graded supplementary readers featuring the most popular guinea pig of them all.	6-7 years
Reading Routes	Longman	144 folders graded by colour into ten levels of difficulty and containing six thematic 'routeways' for optional variety of organization. Answer cards, workbooks and target scoring sheets.	7-12+ years
Seven Silly Stories	Longman	7 full colour stories with a 'folk tale' flavour.	6-7 years
Publisher	Oliver & Boyd, Croythorn House, 23 Ravelston Terrace, Edinburgh, EH4 3JJ		
Flamingo Books	Oliver & Boyd	32 extension readers with controlled vocabulary and sentence structure.	6-11 years
Trug Books	Oliver & Boyd	12 supplementary readers.	5-6 years
Pedro Books	Oliver & Boyd	Supplementary readers that follow Trug books.	6-7 years

Reading materials	Publisher	Brief description	Reading age
Dominoes	Oliver & Boyd	Five stages, six titles per stage.	Pre-reading to 6 years
Happy Venture	Oliver & Boyd	Combines phonic and sentence methods. Carefully graded.	Pre-reading to 8 years
Wide Range Interest Readers	Oliver & Boyd	Two parallel series of graded readers. Accompanied by Quiz Books and Interest Readers.	7-11 years
Publisher	Ginn and Co. Ltd, Elsinore House, Buckingham Street, Aylesbury, HP20 2NQ		
Approach Trend	Ginn	For failing and reluctant readers in upper primary and secondary schools.	$6\frac{1}{2}$-7 years
Trend Mainstream	Ginn	For failing and reluctant readers in upper primary and secondary schools.	7-$9\frac{1}{2}$ years
Trend	Ginn	For failing and reluctant readers in secondary schools only.	10-14 years
Trend Basic Literacy Programme 1: Book Kit (Trend and Approach Trend Books)	Ginn	33 titles for failing readers in upper primary and secondary schools; 1 Trend wall chart.	$6\frac{1}{2}$-$7\frac{1}{2}$ years

Title	Publisher	Description	Age
Trend Basic Literacy Programme 1: Resources K t	Ginn	Teaching-to-read material for failing readers in upper primary and secondary schools — 226 double-sided activity cards and 3 magazine-style lift-outs (*Hi, Kids!, What a Bike* and *Red Hot Rocket*); 1 Trend wall chart; 1 Trend Teachers' Manual.	$6\frac{1}{2}$-$7\frac{1}{2}$ years
Rescue Stories	Ginn	Remedial readers. Activity material also available.	7-$8\frac{1}{2}$ years
More Rescue Stories		Vocabulary a little more extensive.	7-$8\frac{1}{2}$ years
Rescue Adventures		Stories a little harder.	9-10 years
Time for Reading	Ginn	Pre-reading to functional literacy.	
Reading 360	Ginn	A balanced and structured skill development programme in 13 levels with teachers' notes.	5-12 years
Magic Circle Books (Reading 360)	Ginn	Enrichment readers for supplementary use.	Lower primary
Phonic Workbooks	Ginn	Effective with any reading scheme.	Use all levels
Ginn Interest Series First Interest	Ginn	20 books graded into 2 levels. 42 titles under six themes.	Early years 7 years approx.
First Interest Library		Non-fiction areas.	7 years approx.
First Interest Activity Cards		Question and experiment-type cards.	7 years approx.

Reading materials	Publisher	Brief description	Reading age
	Ernest Benn Ltd, Sovereign Way, Tonbridge, Kent, TN9 1RW		
Beginning to Read Books	Benn	Stories.	9-11 years
Inner Ring Books	Benn	Restricted vocabulary.	7-8 years
Jimmy Books	Benn	Restricted vocabulary.	9-12 years
	Blackie & Son Ltd, Western Cleddens Road, Bishopbriggs, Glasgow, GG4 2NZ		
Sparks	Blackie	Six-stage reading scheme.	Pre-reading to 8 years
Focus Books	Blackie	Restricted vocabulary.	8-9 years
Kaleidoscope Books	Blackie	Chosen topics.	8-9 years
Kennett Library	Blackie	Stories.	10-11 years
My Five Senses	Blackie	Factual.	6-8½ years
Phoenix Library	Blackie	Stories.	10-12 years
Pictures and Words	Blackie	Basic reading material.	5+

Title	Publisher	Description	Age range
Read, Write and Remember	Blackie	For slow readers.	6-8 years
True Adventure Series	Blackie	Factual stories.	8-9 years
Publisher	W. & R. Chambers Ltd, 11 Thistle Street, Edinburgh, EH2 1DG		
Quest Books	Chambers	Stories.	7-11 years
Young Set Dictionaries	Chambers	Graded primary dictionaries.	3-12 years
Publisher	Macmillan Publishers Ltd, 4 Little Essex Street, London, WC2R 3LF		
Look (Jackson & Reeve)	Macmillan	Visual perception materials: Teachers' Book Workbooks Master Stencil Book.	
Colourwise (Smith) 6 titles	Macmillan	Bright paperback booklets to help in naming and identifying colours.	4-7 years
Gay Way (Boyce)	Macmillan	6 levels of Basic Readers, Auxillary and Supplementary Readers plus workbooks.	5-7+ years
Nippers (ed. Leila Berg) 68 titles	Macmillan	5 levels of bright, contemporary reading books.	6-8+ years
Little Nippers 20 titles	Macmillan		5-7 years
Club 75 (ed. Aiden Chambers) 12 titles	Macmillan	Upper Primary — each book contains full story.	10-13 years

Reading materials	Publisher	Brief description	Reading age
Varieties (Tate)	Macmillan	Short lively stories for the slower, older reader in the primary school.	8-11 years
Language in Action	Macmillan	First scheme based on constituent parts of English language. Comprehensive Level 0; Pre-Literacy Levels 1, 2, 3; Basic Language Structures. Language Guides.	5-8 years
Crown St. Kings (Oates) 18 titles	Macmillan	For upper primary pupils with reading age between 8-9 years.	Interest 10-12 years Reading level 8-9 years
Words for Topics	Macmillan	Valuable aid to spelling, reading and writing; visual.	5-8 years
First Topic Books 6 titles	Macmillan	Junior environmental studies about 'How Things are Made'.	5-8 years
Publisher	McGraw Hill Book Co. (UK) Ltd, Shoppenhangers Road, Maidenhead, SL6 2QL		

Title	Publisher	Description	Level
Programmed Reading (Sullivan & Buchanan) Visual material (for use with Reading Readiness & Series 1) Alphabet Strips Cards (set of 29) Teacher Alphabet Cards Pupil Alphabet Cards	McGraw-Hill	Reading Programme containing the following: 1. Pupil response booklets 2. Teachers' guides 3. Achievement tests 4. Word cards 5. Filmstrips 6. Webstermasters 7. Storybooks	Nursery to junior secondary
Reading for Concepts (Liddle) 8 titles	McGraw-Hill	Non-fiction storybooks. Tape cassette programme.	Lower to upper primary
New Practice Readers (Stone)	McGraw-Hill	High interest stories. Answer pads.	Low-middle primary
The Every Reader Series (Kottmeyer) Adventures in English series	McGraw-Hill	Adaptations of classics for reluctant readers.	10-18 years
Read and Think Series (Sullivan & Buchanan)	McGraw-Hill	Early primary story books.	
Tell Again Story Cards (Scott)	McGraw-Hill	Picture cards for building listening skills.	

Reading materials	Publisher	Brief description	Reading age
Publisher	Thomas Nelson & Sons Ltd, Windmill Road Sunbury-on-Thames Middlesex TW16 7HP		
Lively Reading	Nelson	Series designed to motivate reluctant readers. Readers, workbooks, teacher's guide. Four levels.	6-10 years Interest age 9-14 years
Livelihoods		Same series style as *Lively Reading*. The simple factual text stimulates and informs while providing good prose.	6-8 years Interest age 11-12 years
Help!	Nelson	Language development course at six levels — First Helpings, Help Story Books, Help Books, Help Yourself, spirit masters, teacher's guide.	6-8 years Interest age 9-14 years
Canal Street	Nelson	Six books including questions and activities. Repetition and carefully controlled vocabulary are the main features.	6-8 years Interest age 8-11 years
Language Stimulus Programme	Nelson	This material is designed to motivate disinterested or functional non-readers. Contains books, sound filmstrips etc.	8-9 years Interest age 9-14 years
Mike and Mandy Readers	Nelson	These stories use carefully controlled vocabulary, natural phrases and simple sentences.	Infant

Skylarks	Nelson	A language development library.	6-9 years
Publisher	Macdonald Educational Publishers Ltd, Holywell House, Worship Street, London, EC2 2EN		
Play School Books	Macdonald	Activity, vocabulary controlled concepts.	3-6 years
Zero Books	Macdonald	Number work, pre-reading illustrations.	3-6 years
Macdonald ABC	Macdonald	Alphabet book.	4-7 years
Starters (all series)	Macdonald	Simple pictures, controlled vocabulary.	5-8 years
Starters Word Book	Macdonald	Reference book for vocabulary used in *Starters*.	5-8 years
Starters Sentences	Macdonald	Companion to Word Book, composing of sentences.	6-8 years
Opposites	Macdonald	Variety of early concepts.	2-6 years
Teaching 5-13	Macdonald	Projects, games for reading.	5-13 years
Using the Environment	Macdonald	Teacher's handbook — outdoor exploration, practical work.	5-13 years
Easy Reading Editions	Macdonald	Designed for children with reading problems.	7-15 years
Countries	Macdonald	Studies all aspects of major countries.	11+ years

Reading materials	Publisher	Brief description	Reading age
Publisher	George Philip Alexander Ltd, Norfolk House, Smallbrook, Queensway, Birmingham, B5 4LJ		
This Is My Sound	George Philip Alexander	Word recognition.	3-6 years
Steps To Reading	George Philip Alexander	Pre-reading.	
Leading To Reading	George Philip Alexander	Pre-reading.	
Laugh and Learn	George Philip Alexander	Illustrated to help identify words.	4-7 years
Publisher	Pergamon Press Ltd, Headington Hill Hall, Oxford, OX3 0BW		
Patterns (Hervey and Walters)	Pergamon Press	Designed for children in need of remedial assistance in upper primary school.	

Publisher	A. Wheaton & Co., Hennock Road, Exeter, EX2 8R2		
Happy Trio Reading Scheme We Read Pictures We Read More Pictures Before We Read We Look & See We Work & Play We Come & Go Guess Who? Fun with Dick & Jane — 1 and 2 Our New Friends — 1 and 2 We Three Friends & Neighbours — 1, 2 and 3 More Friends & Neighbours — 1 and 2 What Next? — 1 and 2 Also available — Think & Do books for above	A. Wheaton & Co.	Progresses through pre-reading skills to a good level of competence.	Infant up
Good Story Readers Books 1-5 (Lamb)	A. Wheaton & Co.	Designed to take children on from the point they reached at the end of the *Happy Trio Reading Scheme*.	8-9 years

Reading materials	Publisher	Brief description	Reading age
More Good Stories Books 1-5 (Lamb)	A. Wheaton & Co.	A series of modern fables.	8-9 years
One Hundred Good Stories Books 1-6 (Lamb)	A. Wheaton & Co.	Includes stories from past and present and 'Things to Do' sections for faster-reading pupils.	9+years
Carford Readers Books 1-8 (Owen)	A. Wheaton & Co.	Remedial readers reflecting familiar family situations.	10+years
Far West Readers (Rudge) Cowboys & Wild Horses / The Ride to Kansas / Stampede in the Valley / Rodeo at Black Rock / Gun Smoke in the Hills / Valley of Gold	A. Wheaton & Co.	Remedial readers, particularly useful with the older child.	10+years
Comprehension & Study Cards Sets 1-4, Answer Books 1-4 (Gregory)	A. Wheaton & Co.	Provides practice in comprehension and basic language skills.	8+years
Lumpo the Baby Elephant (Gibbons)	A. Wheaton & Co.	Story books for young children.	Infant
Berry House Books (Clarke) 10 books	A. Wheaton & Co.	Infant readers with the Berry family and their pets as the centre of interest.	Infant

I Can Help Myself (Forster) Books 1-4	A. Wheaton & Co.	Remedial books for young children.	Infant
Pointers (Garvey)	A. Wheaton & Co.	Set of twenty-four writing and project cards. Includes teacher's card.	11 years
Highway to Understanding (Richards)	A. Wheaton & Co.	Contains sixty extracts from well known books followed by a series of questions designed to test the pupil's understanding.	
Read & Discover (Taylor) Books 1 and 2	A. Wheaton & Co.	Designed to provide practice in reading, comprehension and creative writing.	10-11 years
Stories from the World: Eagle of Gwerraby; Stray Cow; Magic & Gold; Kunegunda; Land of the Locust Tree	A. Wheaton & Co.	Series of folk tales from Wales, Northern Europe, Poland and China.	10-11 years
Read About It Series (Gregory) Books 1-72 and 97-120	A. Wheaton & Co.	Provides simple, reliable information on a wide range of subjects for young children or backward readers.	
The Poet's Sphere (Bricknell Smith)	A. Wheaton & Co.	Thematic presentation of over 300 poems by poets.	10+years
Twenty Narrative Poems (Bricknell Smith)	A. Wheaton & Co.	Includes both classical and modern poems of the genre.	10+years

Reading materials	Publisher	Brief description	Reading age
Publisher	Methuen & Co. Ltd, 11 New Fetter Lane, London, EC4P 4EE		
Ready to Read Scheme	Methuen	*Little Books*	$5\frac{1}{2}$-$6\frac{1}{2}$ years
		Stage 1	
		Large Books	
		Stage 2	$6\frac{1}{4}$-$7\frac{1}{4}$ years
		Stage 3	$7\frac{1}{4}$-$8\frac{1}{2}$ years
		Stage 4	8-12 years
		Full colour illustrated story books.	
Caption Books	Methuen	Red, Yellow and Blue Series	5-$5\frac{1}{2}$ years
		Green Series	$5\frac{1}{2}$-6 years
		Purple Series	6-$6\frac{1}{2}$ years
		Orange Series	$6\frac{1}{4}$-7 years
Terraced House Books	Methuen	Full colour photographs.	$5\frac{1}{2}$-6 years
Instant Readers	Methuen	Black and white photographs.	5-$5\frac{1}{2}$ years
Read it Yourself Books	Methuen	Set A	$5\frac{1}{2}$-6 years
		Set B	6-$6\frac{1}{2}$ years
Do You Know This Word Books	Methuen		$5\frac{1}{2}$-6 years

REFERENCES

Reading in the Primary School

1   James A. Smith, *The Creative Teaching of Reading and Literature in Elementary School*, (Allyn & Bacon, 1975).
2   Herbert Kohl, *Reading, How to,* p.146 (Penguin, 1974).
3   Tom Nicholson, *An Anatomy of Reading*, p.i. (Research and Planning Branch, Education Department, South Australia, 1973).

Chapter 2   Reading Readiness
1   J. Downing and D.V. Thackray, *Reading Readiness*, p.89 (Hodder & Stoughton, 2nd edn 1975).
2   Marie Clay, *Reading: The Patterning of Complex Behaviour*, p.36 (Heinemann Educational, 1972).
3   Tom Nicholson, op. cit., p.23.
4   Marie Clay, op. cit., p.165.
5   Tom Nicholson, op. cit., p.71.
6   Marie Clay, op. cit., p.14.
7   Marie Clay, op. cit., p.28.
8   ibid.
9   Marie Clay, op. cit., p.60.
10   Tom Nicholson, op. cit., p.24.
11   Marie Clay, op. cit., p.74.
12   Marie Clay, op. cit., p.75.
13   ibid.
14   Marie Clay, op. cit., p.110.
15   Tom Nicholson, op. cit., p.26.

Chapter 3   The Initial Teaching of Reading
1   Donald Moyle, *The Teaching of Reading*, p.25 (Ward Lock Educational, 4th edn, 1976).
2   W.S. Gray, *The Teaching of Reading and Writing: An International Survey*, (UNESCO, Paris, 1973).
3   Marie Clay, op. cit., p.165.
4   ibid.
5   Brenda Thompson, *Learning to Read: A Guide for Teachers and Parents*, p.103 (Sidgwick & Jackson, 1970).
6   Reprinted from articles by Julie Biles in *Primary Education* magazine, Vol.5, No.2.
7   Mary Anne Hall, *Teaching Reading as a Language Experience* (Charles E. Merrill Publishing Company).
8   ibid.

9   Robert B. Buddell, 'Reading Instruction in First Grade with Varying Emphasis on the Regularity of Grapheme-Phoneme Correspondences and the Relation of Language Structure to Meaning — Extended into Second Grade', *The Reading Teacher*, XX (May 1967).

10   Maureen Applegate, *Easy in English* (Row, Paterson & Co., 1962).

11   Robert Rosenthal and Lenore Jacobson, *Pygmalion in the Classroom* (Holt, Rinehart & Winston, 1968).

12   Robert Barret, 'The Relationship between Measures of Pre-reading Visual Discrimination and First-Grade Reading Achievement', *Reading Research Quarterly*, February 1965.

13   Mary Anne Hall, op. cit.

14   C.A. Lefevre, *Linguistics and the Teaching of Reading* (McGraw-Hill, 1964).

15   Leonard Bloomfield and Clarence L. Barnhart, *Let's Read, A Linguistic Approach* (Wayne State University Press, 1961).

16   C.C. Fries, *Linguistics and Reading* (Holt, Rinehart & Winston, 1963).

17   Leonard Bloomfield, *A Linguistic Approach to Teaching Reading* (Wayne State University Press, 1961).

Chapter 4   The Dependent Reader

1   James A. Smith, op. cit., p.23.

2   N.B. Smith, *Reading Instruction for Today's Children*, p.210 (Prentice-Hall, 1964).

3   Tom Nicholson, op. cit., p.147.

4   Herbert Kohl, op. cit., p.65.

5   Wallace Hildick, *Children and Fiction*, pp.78 and 80 (Evans, 1970).

6   Wallace Hildick, op. cit., p.81.

Chapter 5   The Independent Reader

1   James A. Smith, op. cit., p.190.

2   Robert Whitehead, *Children's Literature: Strategies of Teaching*, p.7 (Prentice-Hall, 1968).

3   James A. Smith, *Adventures in Communication*, p.288 (Allyn & Bacon, 1972).

4   C.S. Huck and D.Y. Kuhn, *Children's Literature in the Elementary School*, p.8 (Holt, Rinehart & Winston, 3rd end 1976).

Chapter 7   Developing a School Reading Programme

1   Tom Nicholson, op. cit., p.148.

2   *The Second International Reading Symposium*, John Downing and Amy L. Brown (eds.), pp.136-9 (Cassell, 1967).

3   John Russell, *Teachers World* (Evans).

4   Brenda Thompson, op. cit., p.106.

5   Herbert Kohl, op. cit., p.161

6   This article first appeared in *Idiom*, the journal of the Victorian Association for the Teaching of English, Australia, and is reprinted with the author's permission.

7   J. Dean and R. Nichols, *Framework for Reading* (Evans, 1974).

8   D. Fader, *Hooked on Books* (Berkley Publishing Corporation, U.S.A., 1966).
9   D. Holdaway, *Independence in Reading* (Ashton Scholastic, available in UK from Better Books, Bath).

Chapter 9   Research and Opinion
1   This paper first appeared in *Occasional Paper Number Nine*, published by the Curriculum and Research Branch of the Education Department, Victoria, Australia, and is reprinted with permission.
2   William S. Tymmes. Foreword. *Dimensions in Learning Disabilities: Indications and Approaches*, p.3.
3   Margaret Clark's paper, 'Language and Reading: Research Trends', appears in *Problems of Language and Learning*, ed. Alan Davies (Heinemann Educational, 1975).
4   Herbert Kohl, op. cit., p.18
5   Vera Southgate, *Educational Research*. Vol.2, No.1, November 1968.
6   James A. Smith, op.cit., p.18.
7   Geoffrey Roberts, *Reading in Primary Schools*, p.32 (Routledge & Kegan Paul, 1969).
8   W.S. Gray, op. cit. p.116.
9   Bond and Dextra, *Reading Research Quarterly*, Australia, 1967.
10   *Forum*, Australia, Spring 1974.
11   Education Department, Western Australia, *Curriculum Report*, 1976.

Chapter 10   Reading Failure
1   This paper first appeared in *The Educational Magazine*, Education Department, Victoria and is reprinted with the author's permission.
2   C.H. Delacato, *The Treatment and Prevention of Reading Problems* (Blackwell, 1959).
3   **M. Frostig and D. Horne, *The Frostig Programme for the Development of visual Perception* (NFER 1964).**
4   Basil Bernstein, *Class, Codes and Control*, Vols.1 and 2 (Routledge and Kegan Paul, 1974 and 1973).
5   **R. Morris, *Success and Failure in Learning to Read* (Penguin, 2nd edn). 1973.**

Appendix B: Reading Materials
1   Ruth Trevor, 'Beginning Reading', *Education*, Vol.19, No.4, September 1970.
2   Herbert Kohl, op. cit., p.57.
3   Marie Clay, op. cit., pp.61-2.
4   Tom Nicholson, op. cit., p.17.
5   Maureen Cullen and Fay Shepherd, Initial Reading Material, *Language Statement* (Curriculum and Research Branch of the Education Department, Victoria, Australia, 1975).

AUTHOR INDEX OF FURTHER READING

Page numbers in italics indicate quotations